# Plant-Based Bean Cookbook

# Plant-Based Bean Cookbook

## 70 VEGAN RECIPES FOR BEAN LOVERS

Edited and with Recipes by Katherine Green

ROCKRIDGE PRESS

Interior and Cover Designer: John Clifford
Art Producer: Tom Hood
Editor: Gleni Bartels
Production Manager: Michael Kay
Production Editor: Mia Moran

Photography © Hélène Dujardin 2021, cover & p. 30; Iain Bagwell, p. ii; Shutterstock, pp vi, vii, viii; bigacis/iStock, p. vii; YelenaYemchuk/iStock, p. x; The Picture Pantry/Stockfood, p. 14; Andrew Purcell, p. 48; Marija Vidal, p. 66; für ZS Verlag/Timmann, Claudia/Stockfood, p. 90; Nadine Greeff, p. 100
Food styling by Anna Hampton, cover & p. 30; Carrie Purcell, p. 48

ISBN: 978-1-64876-972-6 | eBook 978-1-64876-280-2
R0

To all the people
striving to improve their health
through dietary changes.

# Contents

# Introduction

Whether you love beans or have a more nuanced relationship with them, there is no denying that they're really good for your body. Cultivated for centuries, beans are one of the oldest plant crops farmed around the world, and they provide sustenance for millions of people every day. But if you didn't grow up loving them or if you've just been subjected to bland bean dishes, you might not hold them in such high esteem, and I can totally relate to that.

My journey with beans began as a child, when lima beans were a regular vegetable on the table. And I hated them. Over the years, my family's bean recipe repertoire grew to include falafel, dal, various bean soups and salads, and more, but I can't say that I really ever liked them until I went away to college and began missing many of those dishes my parents used to prepare at home. I slowly began to make them on my own as a way to feel closer to my family, and by the time I started my own family, my love for the humble legume had really begun to take shape.

Whether you follow a plant-based diet or are just looking to add more plant-based meals to your menu, beans are a wonderful and inexpensive protein to prepare for just about any meal. This book will introduce you to 70 recipes featuring the most common 18 beans and how to serve them. Whether you are a lifelong carnivore or an experienced plant-based eater, my hope is that some of the recipes contained in these pages can become part of your tried-and-true plant-based meal collection.

## How to Use This Book

Many recipes in this book call for cooked beans. For these, refer to the Bean Cooking Quick Reference Guide (see page 101) for the cooking times to prepare beans from scratch on the stovetop, in a pressure cooker, or in a slow cooker, or you can substitute canned beans in their place.

While each recipe in this book highlights one or more bean types, feel free to switch things up to work with what you have in your kitchen and to suit your own personal tastes. Because there are variables like using canned or dried beans or store-bought or homemade broth (see page 92) in the recipes, many are only lightly salted to ensure the end product is not overly salty. Be sure to taste and add more salt and pepper as needed to suit your tastes or dietary preferences.

## CHAPTER ONE

# BEAN BASICS

Before we get started on the recipes, let's go over the basics. In this chapter, we will look at all the different beans used in the recipes in this book and learn about the best ways to prepare them. By the end of this chapter, you'll be ready to dive into the recipes and get cooking with confidence.

# A HUMBLE POT OF BEANS

Beans have been around for thousands of years and are part of the same family (Fabaceae) as legumes and pulses. Though the names are often used interchangeably, all three terms have distinct meanings. *Legume* refers to the leaves, stems, or pods of any plant belonging to the Fabaceae family, while *pulses* are the edible seeds from legume plants, such as peas, beans, and lentils. Different types of beans, like chickpeas, white beans, black beans, and pinto beans, are pulses but are commonly referred to as beans.

Beans are extremely versatile and can be served for just about any meal: They can form the backbone of many different types of soups and stews, from the simple Cranberry Bean Minestrone Soup (page 52) where they accompany many vegetables to the blended Spicy Black Bean Soup (page 51) where they are the star. They can be a side dish, like the Roasted Garlic Green Beans (page 32) and Thyme and Garlic Cranberry Beans (page 36), or a main dish like Mung Bean Dal (page 70) or Pinto Bean and Cremini Mushroom Burritos with Cilantro Sour Cream (page 85). They can even be used in sweet dishes, like the Chocolate Chip Chickpea Blondies (page 98) or the Vanilla Date Shake (page 96).

They're also incredibly budget-friendly. In most places, one-pound bags of dried beans cost less than a dollar and will provide enough food for multiple meals. If saving time in the kitchen is important, canned beans are a cheap option to create quick, filling meals that can be ready in minutes. Best of all, with a little imagination and a few varieties of beans in your pantry, you can whip up everything from delicious side dishes to entrées to desserts.

# PLANT-POWERED HEALTH

Beans are the most bang-for-the-buck food around, especially when it comes to nutrition. Numerous studies have proven the health benefits of eating beans, including:

**Protein without the cholesterol.** A ½ cup serving of beans has about 7 grams of protein—the highest amount of protein of all plants—without the cholesterol of meats. Protein is necessary for the production of hormones and the growth and repair of bones, nerves, and tissues. Because most beans are missing one of the eight amino acids, methionine, they're often paired with rice or bread to make a complete protein that can provide enough protein for the body's needs on a vegetarian diet.

**Fiber for satiation.** The journal *Food & Nutrition Research* concluded that people who consume plant-based meals using beans and peas stayed fuller longer than those who ate animal-based, high-protein meals with similar calorie and protein content. The reason for this is fiber, which takes longer to digest and provides volume, which helps you stay fuller for longer. Fiber is present in vegetables, fruit, and whole grains and is an important part of a healthy diet.

**Low fat.** Unlike other protein sources, such as dairy and meat, most beans are low in fat and are cholesterol free. Fat and cholesterol are both needed in the body for healthy function, but there are "good" and "bad" cholesterol and fats. Unsaturated fats, like the kind found in soybeans and the vegetable oils used in these recipes, are a good type of fat when used in moderation, while saturated fats, like those found in meats and dairy products, should be limited to reduce the risk of cardiovascular disease.

**Plenty of micronutrients.** Beans are rich in magnesium, calcium, and phosphorus, all key components in the health of bones and teeth, muscle function, normalizing blood sugar levels, and maintaining a healthy immune system. Beans also contain potassium, a necessary mineral that helps the kidneys work efficiently and lowers blood pressure. Zinc, a mineral that helps wounds heal and is critical for a healthy immune system, is present in legumes. Beans are rich in B vitamins and folate as well as antioxidants, which help neutralize free radicals in the body.

**Prevention of disease.** Eating just one serving of beans per day has been shown to help lower LDL ("bad") cholesterol, whereas four servings per week can lower your risk of heart disease and decrease the risk of colon cancer.

## About the Plant-Based Diet

All the recipes in this book follow the basics of a plant-based diet, one that is made up primarily of fruits, vegetables, whole grains, and legumes. The plant-based diet is defined in a few different ways, from not eating any animal products or processed foods to a more general approach of eating mostly plant-based foods with occasional meat or processed foods.

However you define "plant-based," the recipes in this book stick to 100 percent plant-based foods with a strong emphasis on whole foods. There will be some lightly processed foods—like whole-grain bread and pasta, tofu, plant-based milk, and canned beans—to help make things easier for everyday cooking, but the recipes all follow this simple definition of plant-based eating.

Some people decide to take the plant-based diet to another level by eliminating salt, oil, and refined sugar, also known as the Whole Food, Plant-Based (or WFPB) Diet. While this book doesn't follow those guidelines, every effort has been made to make these recipes as healthy as possible while still having tons of flavor. Since not everyone at your table will have the same dietary restrictions, there are tips on ways to experiment with the recipes to make them suitable for vegetarians and meat eaters, too.

Recipes also include labels to indicate recipes that are friendly with other diets, such as gluten-free, nut-free, oil-free, and soy-free. As always, be sure to check ingredient labels to make sure they are safe for your diet—including plant-based products, which often include ingredients derived from wheat, nuts, and soy.

## KNOW YOUR BEAN TYPES

There are over 400 types of beans in the world, but this book covers 18 of the most beloved varieties, which are pretty common and accessible at major grocery stores and smaller markets. These include:

**Adzuki bean:** These small red beans are popular in Asian cuisines and have a slightly nutty flavor. They are often used in sweet dishes but also work well in soups, rice dishes, and salads. Look for adzuki beans at specialty stores, Asian grocery stores, and online.

**Black bean:** Also known as black turtle beans, black beans are used in many Latin American dishes. Their firm, meaty texture makes them great for soups, salads, and fillings. Be sure to rinse black beans well before using in salads and colorful dishes, as the cooking liquid will color the dish black otherwise.

**Black-eyed pea:** These distinctive, earthy-flavored beans are easy to spot with their creamy color and black spot. They are sometimes called cow peas, though they are not a pea at all. They hold special significance in the soul food of the American South and symbolize prosperity.

**Cannellini bean:** A common white bean that is often found canned, the cannellini bean is actually a white kidney bean. Like the kidney bean, dried cannellini beans should be soaked and then boiled for 10 minutes before simmering. These can be used interchangeably with navy and great northern beans in baked beans, salads, dips, and soups.

**Chickpea:** Also called garbanzo beans, chickpeas are roundish and wrinkled, unlike other beans, which are smooth. The most common variety is tan, but they also come in black, red, white, and brown. They are used in hummus, falafel, salads, stews, and many other dishes from cuisines throughout the world as both a main course and side dish.

**Cranberry bean:** Also called borlotti beans, cranberry beans have a striking appearance with their speckled red or magenta color. They are a medium to large bean, and though they look lovely when dried, they lose their color during the cooking process.

**Fava bean:** Known also as broad beans, fava beans are widely used in Middle Eastern and Mediterranean cooking. Preparing them from fresh requires shelling, blanching, and peeling the beans, but the end result is worth the work. Dried fava beans must be soaked overnight, but buying ones that have been peeled eliminates the additional work.

**Gigante bean:** This large, flat, white bean variety is native to the Mediterranean and Greece. Gigante beans are actually an extra-large runner bean and are great stewed and in salads. They are not widely available but can be found online, dried or cooked in cans or jars.

**Great northern bean:** These are a common white bean that can be used interchangeably with cannellini beans or navy beans. They are smaller than the cannellini bean but larger than the navy bean, making them a good choice for soups, casseroles, and salads.

**Green bean:** These are the immature, young versions of common beans in their pods, differentiating them from other mature beans removed from their pods. String beans, snap beans, and French beans are common names, and they are sold fresh, frozen, and canned.

**Kidney bean:** Commonly called red beans, these are available in both large and small varieties. Small red beans are common in Creole cuisine. Kidney beans contain a toxin that is destroyed through cooking, so be sure to soak and then boil the beans for at least 10 minutes at the beginning of cooking.

**Lentil:** Originating in the Middle East, lentils are a diet staple throughout the world and thought to be the oldest cultivated legume. There are several varieties available; the most common types are brown, green, le Puy, yellow, and red. They are quick-cooking and do not require soaking, though soaking can decrease the cook time further.

**Lima bean:** While they are both the same bean, in culinary use, *lima bean* refers to the young green bean, while *butter bean* is the name for the older, larger, yellow-beige-colored bean. Look for dried, canned, and/or frozen lima beans.

**Mung bean:** This legume is cultivated throughout East Asia, the Indian subcontinent, and Southeast Asia and is also known as green gram or moong. It is used in soups, curries, and salads as well as sweet dishes. Mung bean sprouts are a popular ingredient in Chinese, Vietnamese, and Korean dishes.

**Navy bean:** A small white bean with a creamy texture, navy beans can be used interchangeably with cannellini and great northern beans. They are commonly used to make baked beans but also work well in salads, dips, and soups.

**Pinto bean:** When dried, the pinto bean is tan with dark speckles. Pinto beans are most often used to make refried beans and chili, and they are a mainstay in Mexican cuisine and Southern cooking in the United States.

**Soybean:** Soybeans have been consumed for thousands of years throughout Asia. Unlike other beans, soybeans contain no starch, making them a great protein choice for diabetics. Edamame, usually eaten whole, are young, green soybeans, while the dried beans are white. Tofu, soymilk, soy sauce, tempeh, and miso are just some of the products made from soybeans.

**Split pea:** *Split pea* simply refers to the dried, peeled, and split-in-half seed of the pea. Green and yellow varieties are commonly available. Both are used to make pea soup, while yellow split peas are used to prepare dal.

## Canned versus Dried

There is no right or wrong way to buy beans. Both dried and canned beans have their advantages. Dried beans are cheaper, can result in a more flavorful dish, and allow you to better control the texture. However, they do require time.

Canned beans, on the other hand, are cheap and require no prep work, making them a great option for a busy day when you don't have time for soaking and cooking. You can open a can and rinse, and they are ready to use.

Here are a few rules of thumb to consider when using canned beans versus dried beans:

- 1 pound of dried beans = 3 to 4 (15-ounce) cans of beans
- 1 (15-ounce) can of beans = 1½ cups of beans
- Always drain and rinse canned beans to remove up to half of the sodium.
- Always buy canned beans labeled "BPA-free."
- Look for low-sodium or no-salt-added canned beans for the best control of sodium in your food.

## SOAKING

Many beans, like kidney beans, black beans, and chickpeas, benefit from soaking to speed things up before you cook them on the stove. Others, like lentils or split peas, don't require soaking, though you can still soak them to reduce cooking time further if desired. Larger beans like gigante beans, lima beans, and fava beans benefit from a greatly reduced cooking time by soaking first.

Before soaking beans, it is important to look through the beans and discard any small rocks or twigs that may be included. Then, depending on how much time you have, you can choose from one of two soaking methods. The traditional way to soak beans is simply to place the beans in a bowl, cover with a few inches of water, and let soak overnight or for 4 to 12 hours, depending on the type of bean. When you are ready to cook the beans, drain the water, rinse with fresh water, and cover the beans with a couple inches of water to cook.

If you wish to speed things up, you can do a quick soak. In this method, you place 3 cups of water for every 1 cup of beans in a large pot and bring the water to a boil for 2 minutes. Turn off the heat, cover, and let rest for an hour. Drain the water, rinse the beans, and cover with water to cook.

## My Top Five Recipes

These are some of my favorite recipes from the book:

1. **Edamame Salsa (page 23):** This fun, bright salsa is a filling snack any time of day and only takes minutes to prepare.
2. **Maple-Glazed Baked Beans (page 34):** This classic side dish is every bit as savory and delicious when made with maple syrup and a simple blend of spices.
3. **Creamy Cauliflower and White Bean Soup with Herbed Croutons (page 57):** Beans and cauliflower create a super creamy base without the dairy, and when topped with homemade croutons, there's a nice contrasting texture.
4. **Buffalo Chickpea Quesadillas (page 78):** The creamy cashew cheese sauce in these is my favorite, and when mixed with Frank's RedHot (or your favorite hot sauce) and chickpeas, it is a simple, flavorful meal.
5. **White Bean, Mushroom, and Kale Potpie (page 86):** There is something so great about a potpie, and this veggie and bean version delivers on the comfort food appeal. The flaky whole-grain crust and saucy vegetables form a great dinner when you have a little more time.

## FLAVORING

There are many ways to get flavor into your beans, and in this section, we'll take a look at what goes into making a pot of beans taste really great.

**Acids:** Lemon and vinegar are two acids commonly used to bring flavor to myriad dishes. However, because they are acidic, when using them with beans, it is best to add them after the beans have softened, as acid can slow the softening process during cooking. The same is true of tomatoes.

**Aromatics:** Vegetables like onions, celery, carrots, and garlic are often included while cooking beans to add a depth of flavor, while herbs like thyme, parsley, and bay leaves build on the flavor even further. When cooking a pound of beans to use in other recipes, I typically use one onion, two garlic cloves, and a bay leaf as a simple yet flavorful base.

**Salt:** While some people swear by salting beans early on, others insist that beans will not get tender during cooking if you add the salt first because the salt can prevent the breakdown of starches in the beans. Typically, I like to add salt when the beans are just barely tender. Sea salt is a good choice. For 1 pound of beans, start with 1 teaspoon of salt and adjust as needed from there.

**Water/broth:** Water or broth can be used for cooking any kind of beans. Broth will give a deeper flavor, but water works just as well, and with the right aromatics, it can be almost indistinguishable from broth. Dried beans will absorb a lot of liquid during cooking, so be sure to cover them with a few inches of liquid and add more as needed throughout the cooking process to keep them covered if the liquid boils down.

## Beans around the World

Beans have been a cornerstone of cuisines around the world for thousands of years. Several recipes in this book, like Mung Bean Dal (page 70), Sesame Chickpeas and Rice (page 71), Baked Black Bean Taquitos (page 19), and Gigante Bean Stew (page 64) draw on inspiration from international cuisines. Let's explore some of the other global approaches to this small but mighty ingredient.

Soybeans are thought to have been domesticated in central China nearly 6,000 years ago and remain a staple in many parts of the world today as products like tofu, tempeh, miso, and soy sauce. In Egypt, where fava beans date back to the days of the pharaohs, a stew called ful medames is the national dish and a popular breakfast item.

Originating in Africa about 5,000 years ago, black-eyed peas are an important sub-Saharan crop due to their ability to thrive in hot, dry conditions. They were grown in ancient Greece and quickly spread to the cuisines of Asia, being used in both Indian and Chinese preparations. Brought to the United States, Brazil, and the Caribbean through the slave trade, black-eyed peas are the star of the traditional Southern dish eaten on New Year's.

Cuban cuisine regularly features *frijoles negros,* a side dish of black beans simmered with bell pepper, onion, cumin, and oregano. Cooking throughout Latin America regularly includes kidney, black, and pinto beans, and they are often served with every meal.

# COOKING

No matter which preparation method you choose, with a few simple steps, you'll always end up with a delicious pot of beans. This section will give you an overview of the different cooking methods and the benefits of each, but for specific preparation times, refer to the Bean Cooking Quick Reference Guide (see page 101) for more detailed information.

## Stovetop

Cooking beans on the stovetop requires no specialized equipment, aside from a heavy-bottomed pot large enough for the beans to swell as they cook. Bring the beans to a boil over high heat; then reduce the heat to low so that the beans simmer gently for the rest of their cooking time. Some beans can take anywhere from 1 to 3 hours to cook, depending on their age, so plan for plenty of time. However, don't increase the heat to try to get the beans cooked quicker—this will just result in the skins breaking and the beans turning into mush. As the beans get close to the desired tenderness, keep an eye on them, since they can quickly overcook.

## Pressure Cooker

The pressure cooker makes cooking dried beans quicker and almost eliminates the need for soaking, since you can just add a little more time to the cooker. If using an electric pressure cooker, opt for the manual setting on high pressure for beans, unless otherwise indicated. For 1 pound of beans, you need a 6- to 8-quart pressure cooker. In the pressure cooker pot, put 1 pound of beans and any aromatics and cover with 8 cups of water. Seal the cooker and cook on high pressure according to the Bean Cooking Quick Reference Guide (see page 101). When the cooking time is up, allow the pressure to release naturally; then open the lid.

## Slow Cooker

A slow cooker is another great hands-off method for cooking beans. When cooking any beans other than lentils, split peas, or mung beans in a slow cooker, be sure to soak them overnight first. The next day, place the beans, any aromatics, and water in the slow cooker. You want to add enough water so that the beans are covered by about 2 inches. Cover the pot and cook on low or high according to the Bean Cooking Quick Reference Guide (see page 101). When cooking a bean type for the first time, check for doneness about 30 minutes before the end of the cooking time and continue checking every 5 to 10 minutes until the beans are tender.

## The Magical Fruit

You're likely familiar with the children's song, but what exactly makes beans such a "magical fruit"? Beans are made up of indigestible carbohydrates, like oligosaccharides, that can't be processed by the digestive enzymes in the stomach and instead pass through the upper intestines to ferment in the lower intestine, causing gas. They're also high in fiber, and increasing fiber in your diet can lead to more gas.

The good news is that your body will eventually adjust to an increase in fiber, and subsequently gas will decrease. One study published in *Nutrition Journal* found that different beans cause different levels of gas, but in all cases, after just eight weeks of eating ½ cup of beans daily, participants' bodies adjusted and returned to normal. If gas is a problem for you as you incorporate more beans into your diet, start with eating small amounts and work your way up as your body adjusts.

If you find that one type of bean always gives you gas, try a different type and you may be surprised that you don't have the same reaction. You can also try cooking beans with spices that have gas-reducing properties, such as cumin, ginger, turmeric, fennel, and sage. If all else fails, there are over-the-counter remedies at both pharmacies and health food stores that can help lessen the effects.

## STORING

Beans are easy and economical, but you can stretch them even further by freezing extra servings for later use. It's helpful to freeze beans in portions typically called for in recipes, generally 1½ to 2 cups, which is about the size of a regular can of beans. Here are some more tips on how to best store beans:

**Cooked beans:** Cooked beans can be stored in the refrigerator for 4 to 5 days. For longer storage, transfer the beans to freezer-safe storage bags or containers and cover with the cooking liquid. Freeze for up to 6 months.

**Dried beans:** Store dried beans in a cool, dry place for up to a year for best quality. They will keep for up to 3 years, but after that they begin to lose nutritional value.

**Fresh beans:** Store fresh unwashed green beans in the refrigerator for up to 7 days.

## LET'S GET COOKING

Now that we've covered the basics, it's time to get cooking. Before you start, here are a few more tips to keep in mind as you cook each batch of beans.

**Experiment with time.** Cooking times for the beans used in these recipes have been provided in the Bean Cooking Quick Reference Guide (see page 101), but the times can vary considerably based on the length of time from harvest ("older" beans will take longer), the type of bean, and the preparation and cooking methods. Altitude can also play a role; beans prepared above 1,000 meters (about 3,300 feet) above sea level will require a longer cooking time due to lower atmospheric pressure. If your beans aren't done, cook them a little longer, and if they are done early, by all means take them off the stove when they are just right.

**Use your bean liquids.** Aquafaba is the name for the liquid that chickpeas or other white beans are cooked with and can be used as a replacement for both eggs and egg whites in recipes. Because of its ability to thicken, emulsify, and bind in recipes, it is widely used in both sweet and savory preparations for people who avoid eggs. Some popular uses include meringue, icing, marshmallows, and mayonnaise.

**Testing for doneness.** Beans can vary in doneness quite a bit, even within one bag or batch, so be sure to always test more than one bean in the pot. I like to make sure at least three beans in a row are tender before taking them off the stove to ensure that they are uniformly cooked.

**Never toss the bean broth.** The water you cooked the beans in is a nutrient-rich and tasty by-product of the cooking process. Use it as a substitute for water or broth or freeze it for later.

CHAPTER TWO

# SNACKS AND SPREADS

< White Bean and Radish Salad on Toast, page 17

# Crispy Toasted Split Peas

MAKES 2 CUPS / PREP TIME: 5 MINUTES, PLUS 15 MINUTES TO SOAK / COOK TIME: 10 MINUTES

5 INGREDIENT / GLUTEN-FREE / NUT-FREE / QUICK / SOY-FREE

Once soaked, split peas can be pan-toasted to crunchy perfection, making these great for everyday munching and snacking or as a crunchy topping on salads. These peas are loaded with protein to keep you feeling full, so skip the chips and grab a handful of this healthy snack instead.

1 cup dried yellow or green split peas

1 tablespoon extra-virgin olive oil

¼ teaspoon salt

½ teaspoon ground cumin

¼ teaspoon sweet paprika

1. In a small saucepan, cover the peas with a couple inches of water. Bring to a boil, and then turn off the heat. Let rest for 15 minutes, until the split peas are visibly swollen. Drain and pat dry with a clean kitchen towel.

2. In a large skillet, heat the oil over medium-high heat. Add the split peas and salt and cook for about 10 minutes, stirring regularly until golden brown and crunchy. Stir in the cumin and paprika and mix well.

3. Transfer to a bowl and cool for several minutes before serving. Store leftovers in an airtight container at room temperature for 2 or 3 days.

**Tip:** Try replacing the cumin and paprika with other spices, like chili powder, garlic powder, curry powder, or dried thyme.

*Per Serving (¼ cup):* Calories: 101; Total fat: 2g; Protein: 7g; Carbohydrates: 16g; Fiber: 7g

# White Bean and Radish Salad on Toast

SERVES 4 / PREP TIME: 10 MINUTES / COOK TIME: 5 MINUTES

NUT-FREE / QUICK / SOY-FREE

White beans are perfect in this salad, where their creamy texture pairs well with the snap of the radishes. Served on slices of crusty toasted bread, this is an easy light meal or snack. Be sure not to skip the step of rubbing the toasts with garlic, as the flavor is really unbeatable.

1½ cups cooked white beans (navy, cannellini, or great northern) or 1 (15-ounce) can, drained and rinsed

8 radishes, sliced

¼ cup chopped fresh parsley

1 jalapeño pepper, seeded and finely chopped

1 tablespoon red wine vinegar

1 tablespoon extra-virgin olive oil, plus more for serving

Salt

Freshly ground black pepper

4 slices whole-grain bread

2 large garlic cloves

1. In a large bowl, mix together the beans, radishes, parsley, jalapeño, vinegar, and oil. Season with salt and pepper.

2. Toast the bread until browned and firm. On a clean work surface, rub the garlic over one side of the toast.

3. Top the toast with the bean salad. Repeat with the remaining toast. Drizzle with oil and season with more salt if desired.

**Tip:** Substitute other herbs, like cilantro, mint, or basil, for the parsley to switch up the flavor profile. For added crunch, add thinly sliced almonds to the radish salad in step 1.

*Per Serving:* Calories: 161; Total fat: 4g; Protein: 8g; Carbohydrates: 25g; Fiber: 7g

# Mung Bean Fritters with Mint Chutney

MAKES 12 FRITTERS / PREP TIME: 15 MINUTES / COOK TIME: 10 MINUTES

NUT-FREE / QUICK / SOY-FREE

Fritters are a fun, unexpected way to include more beans in your diet. These Indian-inspired, panfried fritters are loaded with flavor. Because of the natural seasonings of ginger, chile, and cilantro, very little, if any, salt is needed to create this delicious finger food.

**FOR THE FRITTERS**

2½ cups cooked mung beans

½ serrano chile, stemmed and seeded

1 tablespoon chopped fresh cilantro

1 teaspoon minced peeled fresh ginger

¼ teaspoon ground cumin

¼ teaspoon garam masala

1 or 2 tablespoons whole wheat flour

Avocado oil, for panfrying

**FOR THE CHUTNEY**

½ cup packed fresh whole mint leaves

¼ cup packed fresh whole cilantro leaves

½ serrano chile, stemmed and seeded

1 tablespoon freshly squeezed lemon juice

¼ teaspoon salt

¼ teaspoon freshly ground black pepper

¼ cup water

1. **MAKE THE FRITTERS:** Place the beans in a blender and pulse several times to coarsely grind.

2. In a medium bowl, combine the ground beans, serrano, cilantro, ginger, cumin, and garam masala. Mix in 1 tablespoon of flour, stir, and, if needed, add the remaining 1 tablespoon of flour, until the batter holds together.

3. In a large skillet, heat about ½ inch of oil over medium-high heat. Drop the batter into the oil by the spoonful. Cook for 2 to 3 minutes, until lightly browned; then flip and cook on the other side, until crisp. Transfer to a paper-towel-lined plate to soak up excess oil. Repeat with the remaining batter.

4. **MAKE THE CHUTNEY:** In a blender, combine the mint, cilantro, serrano, lemon juice, salt, and pepper. Add the water and blend until smooth. Serve the fritters with the chutney for dipping.

**Tip:** A lot of the heat of a chile pepper is concentrated in its seeds and ribs, so removing these is essential to keeping the heat level down. If you have a particularly hot serrano or are not a fan of spicy foods, use just half of what is called for here to create a mild heat.

*Per Serving (3 fritters):* Calories: 145; Total fat: 1g; Protein: 9g; Carbohydrates: 27g; Fiber: 10g

# Baked Black Bean Taquitos

SERVES 4 / PREP TIME: 15 MINUTES / COOK TIME: 25 MINUTES

GLUTEN-FREE / NUT-FREE / SOY-FREE

Making taquitos in the oven is super easy and also cuts down on the fat you'd use to fry them. Plus, when you make them at home, you know what goes in the recipe and can control the ingredients. This is a simple recipe, but feel free to add chopped jalapeño pepper, Plant-Based Sour Cream (page 93), and chopped scallions for serving or inside the tortillas as you prefer.

1½ cups cooked black beans or 1 (15-ounce) can, drained and rinsed

1 (4-ounce) can diced green chiles, drained

½ teaspoon garlic powder

½ teaspoon onion powder

¼ teaspoon salt

¼ teaspoon freshly ground black pepper

8 (6-inch) corn tortillas

Olive oil cooking spray

Salsa, for serving

1. Preheat the oven to 375°F.
2. In a small bowl, combine the beans, chiles, garlic powder, onion powder, salt, and pepper. Using a fork, mash the beans until few pieces remain.
3. Cover the tortillas with a damp paper towel and heat in the microwave for about 20 seconds, until pliable. Place the tortillas on a clean work surface.
4. Spread each tortilla with a couple tablespoons of bean mixture in the center; then roll up. Use a dollop of beans to seal the tortilla shut; then transfer, seam-side down, to the baking sheet. Repeat with the remaining tortillas.
5. Spray all the tortillas with cooking spray and bake for 20 to 25 minutes, until crispy. Serve with salsa for dipping.

**Tip:** For meat eaters in your house, add a couple tablespoons of cooked shredded chicken to each tortilla in step 4.

*Per Serving:* Calories: 200; Total fat: 2g; Protein: 9g; Carbohydrates: 39g; Fiber: 9g

# Adzuki and Mushroom Meatballs in Marinara

MAKES 15 / PREP TIME: 20 MINUTES / COOK TIME: 40 MINUTES
FREEZABLE / GLUTEN-FREE / NUT-FREE / SOY-FREE

Mushrooms are a savory addition that produce a really meaty flavor in dishes like this one. These bean-and-mushroom "meat" balls are a nice appetizer, or if you pair them with pasta, they can be served as a meatless main. A quick homemade marinara sauce is included for serving, but feel free to substitute your favorite store-bought version for ease.

**FOR THE MEATBALLS**

Olive oil cooking spray

1½ cups cooked adzuki beans or 1 (15-ounce) can, drained and rinsed

8 ounces cremini mushrooms, sliced

2 tablespoons extra-virgin olive oil

1 small onion, finely chopped

3 garlic cloves, chopped

¾ cup Everyday Vegetable Broth (page 92) or store-bought low-sodium broth

¾ cup rolled oats

¼ cup chopped fresh parsley

1 teaspoon dried oregano

½ teaspoon salt

1. Preheat the oven to 400°F. Line a baking sheet with parchment paper and spray with cooking spray. Set aside.

2. **MAKE THE MEATBALLS:** In a food processor, combine the beans and mushrooms and pulse until coarsely chopped.

3. In a large skillet, heat the oil over medium-high heat. Add the onion and cook for about 3 minutes, until starting to soften. Add the mushroom-bean mixture and cook for about 3 more minutes, until lightly browned. Add the garlic and cook for about 30 seconds, until fragrant. Add the broth, oats, parsley, oregano, and salt and mix well. Stir for about 1 minute, until the liquid is absorbed.

4. Using a spoon, take a heaping tablespoon of the mixture and form it into a 2-inch ball. Place on the prepared baking sheet and continue until all the mixture is formed into balls, making about 15 balls. Spray the tops of the balls with cooking spray. Bake for 25 to 30 minutes, until firm and browned.

**FOR THE MARINARA**

2 tablespoons extra-virgin olive oil

2 garlic cloves, smashed

1 (15-ounce) can crushed tomatoes

½ cup water

1 tablespoon chopped fresh basil

½ teaspoon dried oregano

¼ teaspoon salt

5. **MAKE THE MARINARA:** While the meatballs bake, prepare the sauce. In a small pot, heat the oil over medium-high heat. Add the garlic and cook for about 30 seconds, until fragrant. Add the tomatoes, water, basil, oregano, and salt. Bring to a boil; then reduce the heat to low. Cover and simmer for about 10 minutes, until the flavors meld. Serve the meatballs with the marinara for dipping.

---

**Tip:** Instead of the marinara, you can make these in a gravy sauce. In a large skillet, heat 3 tablespoons of olive oil and stir in 3 tablespoons of whole wheat flour. Stir in 2 cups of vegetable broth. Bring to a simmer and cook for 3 to 4 minutes, until thickened. If desired, stir in a bit of unsweetened almond milk for a creamy gravy, or serve plain, seasoned with salt and pepper.

*Per Serving (3 meatballs):* Calories: 285; Total fat: 12g; Protein: 10g; Carbohydrates: 37g; Fiber: 9g;

# Easy Chickpea Flatbreads

MAKES ABOUT 12 FLATBREADS / PREP TIME: 5 MINUTES / COOK TIME: 25 MINUTES

5 INGREDIENT / GLUTEN-FREE / NUT-FREE / OIL-FREE / QUICK / SOY-FREE

These flatbreads come together in just a few minutes and are great alongside salads or for scooping up dips, such as Edamame Salsa (page 23), Vibrant Beet Hummus (page 26), or Tangy Cheeze Dip (page 24). If you have a good nonstick skillet, you can keep these oil-free, but you can also add a little olive oil to the pan if desired.

**FOR THE DRY MIX**

1½ cups chickpea flour

1½ teaspoons nutritional yeast

1 teaspoon onion powder

¾ teaspoon salt

½ teaspoon baking soda

**FOR THE BATTER**

3 cups water

¼ cup freshly squeezed lemon juice

1. **MAKE THE DRY MIX:** In a jar with a tight-fitting lid, combine the flour, nutritional yeast, onion powder, salt, and baking soda. Close the jar and shake well to combine thoroughly.

2. **MAKE THE BATTER:** In a medium bowl, whisk together the dry mix, water, and lemon juice.

3. Heat a large nonstick skillet over medium-high heat. Once hot, pour ¼ cup of the batter into the center of the pan. Using the back of a soup spoon, immediately swirl the batter out in a circular motion so that your flatbread is round(ish), thin, and uniform in thickness.

4. Once the flatbread has bubbles on top and looks dry around the edges, flip it. Cook until the other side is golden brown. This should be a fairly quick process, about 1 minute per side. Transfer to a plate.

5. Repeat until the batter is used up. Store leftover flatbreads in an airtight container in the refrigerator for up to 3 days.

**Tip:** These take a little practice to form into round flatbreads in the pan, but I say "round(ish)" in the instructions for a reason—there's no need to get all perfectionist with these things. As long as they're (relatively) flat and not too thick, they'll be fine. If your batter becomes too thick at any point, whisk in a bit more water.

*Per Serving (1 flatbread):* Calories: 53; Total fat: 1g; Protein: 4g; Carbohydrates: 8g; Fiber: 2g

# Edamame Salsa

This bright green edamame salsa is a fun take on pico de gallo. It is a protein- and veggie-rich snack that will keep you full longer than a tomato-based salsa. Serve it with your favorite pita chips, tortilla chips, or crackers.

1 cup steamed shelled edamame, cooled

1 cup chopped cucumber

1 cup quartered cherry tomatoes

¼ cup chopped red onion

Juice of 1 lime

½ jalapeño pepper, seeded and minced

2 garlic cloves, minced

1 teaspoon salt

In a large bowl, mix together the edamame, cucumber, tomatoes, onion, lime juice, jalapeño, garlic, and salt. Serve immediately or chill for 1 hour before serving.

**Tip:** Edamame is the only vegetable that contains all nine essential amino acids, making it a great food to add to your diet.

*Per Serving (½ cup):* Calories: 49; Total fat: 1g; Protein: 4g; Carbohydrates: 7g; Fiber: 2g

# Tangy Cheeze Dip

**MAKES ABOUT 2 CUPS / PREP TIME: 10 MINUTES**

GLUTEN-FREE / NO COOK / OIL-FREE / QUICK / SOY-FREE

This "cheesy" dip is deliciously creamy, high in fiber, and low in fat. Use it in wraps and sandwiches or just plain as a dip for raw cucumbers, celery, crackers, Easy Chickpea Flatbreads (page 22), or tortilla chips. If you don't have a high-speed blender, soak the cashews for a few hours beforehand, or boil them for 10 minutes and then drain them before using so that they're soft enough to blend smooth.

1½ cups cooked white beans (cannellini, navy, or great northern) or 1 (15-ounce) can, drained and rinsed

¼ cup nutritional yeast

¼ cup raw unsalted cashew pieces

¼ cup roasted red peppers

2 tablespoons freshly squeezed lemon juice

2 tablespoons water

2 garlic cloves

½ teaspoon salt

In a blender, combine the beans, nutritional yeast, cashews, roasted red peppers, lemon juice, water, garlic, and salt. Blend for about 1 minute, until very smooth and velvety. Serve cold or at room temperature. Store in an airtight container in the refrigerator for 3 to 5 days.

*Per Serving (½ cup):* Calories: 257; Total fat: 5g; Protein: 20g; Carbohydrates: 37g; Fiber: 11g

# Black Bean Dip with Plantain Chips

SERVES 5 / PREP TIME: 15 MINUTES / COOK TIME: 30 MINUTES

GLUTEN-FREE / NUT-FREE / SOY-FREE

Plantains are another great choice for dipping, as they cook to crispy really nicely to make a firm chip. Cut the chips on the bias, or diagonally, so they have as much surface area as possible for dipping. When the chips are paired with this spicy black bean dip, this is one plant-based snack that you can feel really good about eating, as it is loaded with vitamins and minerals to support your health.

**FOR THE PLANTAIN CHIPS**

2 green plantains, peeled and cut on the bias into ¼-inch slices

2 tablespoons extra-virgin olive oil

**FOR THE BLACK BEAN DIP**

1½ cups cooked black beans or 1 (15-ounce) can, drained and rinsed

¼ cup coarsely chopped cilantro

¼ cup chopped scallions, green and white parts, divided

½ jalapeño pepper, seeded and coarsely chopped

Juice from 1 lime

2 tablespoons extra-virgin olive oil

¼ teaspoon ground cumin

¼ teaspoon freshly ground black pepper

1. **MAKE THE PLANTAIN CHIPS:** Preheat the oven to 350°F. Line a baking sheet with parchment paper.

2. In a large bowl, toss the plantains with the oil and arrange on the prepared baking sheet in a single layer.

3. Bake for 15 minutes; then flip and bake for about 15 more minutes, until crispy.

4. **MAKE THE BLACK BEAN DIP:** Meanwhile, in a food processor or blender, combine the beans, cilantro, half of the scallions, the jalapeño, lime juice, oil, cumin, and pepper. Process until just barely smooth with a few pieces remaining.

5. Transfer the dip to a bowl and garnish with the remaining scallions. Serve with the plantain chips for dipping. Store in an airtight container in the refrigerator for 3 to 5 days.

**Tip:** Swap out the jalapeño for a chipotle chile with adobo sauce for a smoky heat instead. To bulk up the recipe a bit more, add tomatoes or corn to the dip after blending it.

*Per Serving:* Calories: 332; Total fat: 2g; Protein: 6g; Carbohydrates: 53g; Fiber: 7g

# Vibrant Beet Hummus

MAKES ABOUT 2½ CUPS / PREP TIME: 10 MINUTES / COOK TIME: 20 MINUTES

5 INGREDIENT / GLUTEN-FREE / NUT-FREE / QUICK / SOY-FREE

This twist on classic hummus is an absolute stunner. It has just enough beet to be a glorious shade of pink—but not so much that it tastes overly earthy or sweet. As such, it's perfection for parties or special events when you really want to impress your guests with something healthy yet pretty and delicious. I like to serve this hummus cold or at room temperature with crackers or raw vegetables.

Olive oil cooking spray

1 small beet, peeled and finely chopped (about 1 cup)

1½ cups cooked chickpeas or 1 (15-ounce) can, drained and rinsed, ½ cup bean liquid reserved

5 tablespoons freshly squeezed lime juice

¼ cup tahini

1 tablespoon extra-virgin olive oil

3 garlic cloves

½ teaspoon salt

1. Preheat the oven to 400°F. Spray a rimmed baking sheet with cooking spray.

2. Scatter the beet cubes on the prepared sheet. Spray the tops lightly with cooking spray and bake for about 20 minutes, until very tender.

3. Transfer the beet cubes to a blender or food processor. Add the chickpeas and reserved liquid, lime juice, tahini, oil, garlic, and salt. Blend until the mixture is velvety smooth. Serve immediately. Store in an airtight container in the refrigerator for 3 to 5 days.

*Per Serving (about ⅓ cup):* Calories: 208; Total fat: 10g; Protein: 8g; Carbohydrates: 25g; Fiber: 7g

# White Bean, Spinach, and Artichoke Dip

SERVES 8 / PREP TIME: 10 MINUTES / COOK TIME: 15 MINUTES

GLUTEN-FREE / NUT-FREE / OIL-FREE / QUICK

This recipe blends cannellini beans with oat milk for a creamy base, but you can use whatever plant-based milk you have on hand. The "cheesy" flavor comes from the combination of yellow miso and nutritional yeast, and while pumpkin may seem like an odd addition, it adds both fiber and a pop of color.

½ onion, sliced

3 garlic cloves, coarsely chopped

1 tablespoon water

1½ cups cooked cannellini beans or 1 (15-ounce) can, drained and rinsed

1 (15-ounce) can pumpkin puree

1 cup unsweetened oat milk

½ cup nutritional yeast

2 tablespoons yellow miso paste

1 tablespoon tapioca starch

1 (1-pound) package chopped frozen spinach

1 (14-ounce) can quartered artichoke hearts, drained

1. In a medium sauté pan or skillet, combine the onion, garlic, and water over high heat. Cook for 3 minutes, or until the onion is translucent and just beginning to brown. Transfer to a blender and add the beans, pumpkin, oat milk, nutritional yeast, miso paste, and tapioca starch. Puree until smooth. Set aside.

2. Return the pan to medium heat and add the spinach. Cook for 4 to 7 minutes, stirring, to thaw the spinach.

3. Stir in the puree mixture. Cook for 3 to 5 minutes, stirring occasionally, until the dip begins to bubble and thicken. Add the artichoke hearts and stir to combine. Serve warm.

4. You can also put the pan, if it's oven-safe, under the broiler for 1 to 2 minutes to give the top layer a little crust and char. Store in an airtight container in the refrigerator for 3 to 5 days.

**Tip:** Use the pulp from an acorn squash instead of the pumpkin for a milder squash flavor.

*Per Serving:* Calories: 147; Total fat: 2g; Protein: 12g; Carbohydrates: 23g; Fiber: 9g

# Refried Lentil Dip

MAKES ABOUT 2 CUPS / PREP TIME: 15 MINUTES / COOK TIME: 20 MINUTES

GLUTEN-FREE / NUT-FREE / OIL-FREE / SOY-FREE

The refried bean texture comes from the food processor or blender because lentils are challenging to mash. Plant-Based Sour Cream (page 93) adds flavor, nutrients, and creaminess. This tastes great warm or cold with chips or pita, on a wrap, or as a dip for crudités.

2 cups water

½ cup dried brown or green lentils, rinsed

1 jalapeño pepper, stemmed

½ cup Plant-Based Sour Cream (page 93) or store-bought

1 (4-ounce) can diced green chiles

1 teaspoon onion powder

½ teaspoon garlic powder

½ teaspoon salt

1. Preheat the broiler.

2. In an 8-quart pot, bring the water to a boil over high heat. Add the lentils, reduce the heat to maintain a simmer, cover the pot, and cook for 15 to 20 minutes. The lentils should be soft and squishable. Drain and set aside.

3. While the lentils cook, wrap the jalapeño in aluminum foil to prevent it from burning. Place it under the broiler for 5 minutes. Turn the jalapeño and cook for 2 minutes more. Remove and set aside.

4. In a high-speed blender or food processor, combine the cooked lentils, roasted jalapeño, sour cream, green chiles, onion powder, garlic powder, and salt. Puree until the dip achieves desired smoothness. Store in an airtight container in the refrigerator for 3 to 5 days.

**Tip:** You can omit roasting the jalapeño pepper, but this step cuts down on the brightness of the pepper and adds more flavor to the dip.

*Per Serving (½ cup):* Calories: 177; Total fat: 7g; Protein: 9g; Carbohydrates: 21g; Fiber: 5g

# SIDES AND SALADS

< Chopped Avocado and Chickpea Salad, page 42

# Roasted Garlic Green Beans

SERVES 4 / PREP TIME: 10 MINUTES / COOK TIME: 20 MINUTES

5 INGREDIENT / GLUTEN-FREE / NUT-FREE / QUICK / SOY-FREE

For the best flavor when making roasted green beans, you want to start with fresh beans that snap easily when bent, not old beans that simply bend. Don't overpack the baking sheet, either—the beans need plenty of space to properly roast and brown nicely.

**1 pound whole green beans, trimmed**

**2 tablespoons extra-virgin olive oil**

**¼ teaspoon salt**

**4 garlic cloves, minced**

1. Preheat the oven to 425°F. Line a baking sheet with parchment paper and set aside.
2. In a large bowl, toss the beans with the oil and salt and arrange in a single layer on the prepared baking sheet. Roast for 12 to 14 minutes, until the beans are nearly crisp-tender and some brown spots have formed.
3. Sprinkle the garlic over the sheet and cook for 2 to 3 more minutes, until the garlic is fragrant. Serve warm.

**Tip:** Lemon zest and/or lemon juice are a good seasoning on roasted green beans. Sprinkle a teaspoon of grated zest and the juice from half a lemon over the beans. For family members who eat dairy, sprinkle a tablespoon of grated Parmesan cheese over each serving.

**Tip:** As an alternative, you can make a green bean casserole instead. To do this, make the Creamy Cashew Sauce (page 94) and sauté 8 ounces of sliced mushrooms for about 8 minutes, until softened and darkened. Mix the cooked mushrooms with the cashew sauce and green beans and combine in a casserole dish. Top with fried onions or bread crumbs and bake for 20 to 25 minutes at 425°F, until bubbly.

*Per Serving:* Calories: 99; Total fat: 7g; Protein: 2g; Carbohydrates: 9g; Fiber: 3g

# Braised Lima Beans

SERVES 6 / PREP TIME: 5 MINUTES / COOK TIME: 20 MINUTES

5 INGREDIENT / GLUTEN-FREE / NUT-FREE / QUICK / SOY-FREE

Using frozen lima beans in this recipe cuts out the prep work of soaking, which makes this dish easy to get on the table for a quick side dish. If you can't find frozen lima beans, use canned lima beans in their place and cut the cook time down to about 10 minutes, until just heated through.

**2 tablespoons extra-virgin olive oil**

**1 sweet onion, minced**

**1 tablespoon smoked paprika**

**1 (12-ounce) bag frozen lima beans**

**½ cup Everyday Vegetable Broth (page 92) or store-bought low-sodium broth**

**Salt**

1. In a large skillet, heat the oil over medium-high heat. Add the onion and paprika and sauté for about 5 minutes, until the onion is softened and browned and the paprika is fragrant.

2. Add the lima beans and broth and bring to a simmer. Cook for 12 to 15 minutes, until the lima beans are tender and the flavors meld. Season with salt and serve.

**Tip:** For a different flavor, replace the smoked paprika with a chopped tomato and a seeded and chopped jalapeño pepper; then simmer as directed.

*Per Serving:* Calories: 129; Total fat: 5g; Protein: 5g; Carbohydrates: 17g; Fiber: 4g

# Maple-Glazed Baked Beans

SERVES 6 / PREP TIME: 15 MINUTES / COOK TIME: 55 MINUTES

GLUTEN-FREE / NUT-FREE / SOY-FREE

Baked beans are a barbecue favorite, and this maple syrup–sweetened version will not disappoint. I tend to use navy beans when making baked beans because I like their smaller size, but any type you have on hand will work in this recipe.

**2 tablespoons extra-virgin olive oil**

**1 onion, chopped**

**3 garlic cloves, minced**

**½ cup pure maple syrup**

**¼ cup tomato paste**

**3 tablespoons apple cider vinegar**

**1 tablespoon vegan Worcestershire sauce**

**1 to 2 teaspoons hot sauce**

**1 teaspoon salt**

**3 cups cooked white beans (cannellini, navy, or great northern) or 2 (15-ounce) cans, drained and rinsed**

1. Preheat the oven to 350°F.
2. In a large skillet, heat the oil over medium-high heat. Add the onion and sauté for 3 to 5 minutes, until softened. Add the garlic and cook for about 30 seconds, until fragrant. Add the maple syrup, tomato paste, vinegar, Worcestershire sauce, hot sauce, and salt and mix well. Stir in the beans and mix well.
3. Transfer the beans to a small baking dish. Cover with aluminum foil and bake for about 45 minutes, until the sauce is thickened and browned around the edges. Serve warm.

**Tip:** To make miso-ginger baked beans, omit the tomato paste, Worcestershire sauce, and hot sauce, and add 2 tablespoons miso paste and 2 teaspoons fresh grated ginger in their place.

**Tip:** If you like, add four slices chopped bacon to the pan in step 2 and cook until brown to give the dish a smoky flavor.

*Per Serving:* Calories: 231; Total fat: 6g; Protein: 7g; Carbohydrates: 39g; Fiber: 6g

# Black-Eyed Peas and Greens

SERVES 6 / PREP TIME: 10 MINUTES / COOK TIME: 1 HOUR 5 MINUTES

GLUTEN-FREE / NUT-FREE / SOY-FREE

Black-eyed peas are a traditional Southern dish served on New Year's Day for good luck. While the beans and greens are typically served separately in the South, this version combines the two in one easy dish. Serve it as a side or pair it with rice for a main course. Black-eyed peas are quicker cooking than other beans, so they can be cooked from dried without soaking, but if you want to save cooking time, you can soak them for just a few hours to speed things up.

2 tablespoons extra-virgin olive oil

1 red onion, chopped

6 garlic cloves, minced

2 cups dried black-eyed peas

6 cups Everyday Vegetable Broth (page 92) or store-bought low-sodium broth

1 bunch collard greens or kale, stemmed and cut into 1-inch pieces

1 teaspoon salt

½ teaspoon freshly ground black pepper

1. In a large pot, heat the oil over medium-high heat. Add the onion and cook, stirring regularly, for about 5 minutes, until softened. Add the garlic and cook for about 30 seconds, until fragrant.

2. Stir in the black-eyed peas and cover with the broth. Bring to a boil; then reduce the heat to low. Cover and simmer for about 45 minutes, stirring occasionally, until the beans are creamy and tender. Add the greens, stir to combine, and continue to cook for 5 to 10 minutes, until tender. Season with salt and pepper and serve.

**Tip:** If you eat meat and want to add more flavor, cook four chopped bacon slices in the pot in step 1 after the onion is cooked.

*Per Serving:* Calories: 290; Total fat: 5g; Protein: 17g; Carbohydrates: 46g; Fiber: 9g

# Thyme and Garlic Cranberry Beans

SERVES 6 / PREP TIME: 5 MINUTES / COOK TIME: 1 HOUR 35 MINUTES

FREEZABLE / GLUTEN-FREE / NUT-FREE / SOY-FREE

Cranberry beans are a creamy bean that works great in a simple side dish like this. This recipe cooks them from dried without soaking, which takes a little extra time but is worth the effort. The garlic is cooked whole here, but when the cooking time is done, it will have fallen apart and melted into the rest of the ingredients to provide wonderful flavor.

**2 tablespoons extra-virgin olive oil**

**4 garlic cloves**

**4 cups water**

**1 cup dried cranberry beans**

**4 sprigs thyme, leaves removed**

**2 bay leaves**

**½ teaspoon salt**

**Red pepper flakes, to taste**

1. In a large saucepan, heat the oil over medium-high heat. Add the garlic and cook for 1 to 2 minutes, until fragrant.

2. Add the water, beans, thyme, and bay leaves. Bring to a simmer and cook for 1 to 1½ hours, until the beans are tender but not mushy. Add more water if the beans begin to dry out toward the end of cooking. Add the salt and red pepper flakes; then serve warm.

**Tip:** If you eat meat, try adding a piece or two of smoked turkey wings or necks to the beans as they cook for added flavor. Before serving, remove the turkey pieces, shred, and return the turkey meat to the pot. Replace the water with chicken broth for an even richer flavor.

*Per Serving:* Calories: 151; Total fat: 5g; Protein: 7g; Carbohydrates: 20g; Fiber: 10g

# Garlicky Kale and White Beans

SERVES 6 TO 8 / PREP TIME: 10 MINUTES / COOK TIME: 10 MINUTES

GLUTEN-FREE / QUICK / SOY-FREE

Since kale is such a nutritional superstar, I try to work it into my diet as much as I can. Here I've paired it with wholesome white beans and a squeeze of fresh lemon juice. Serve it topped with Plant-Based Parmesan (page 95) for even more flavor.

2 tablespoons extra-virgin olive oil

2 teaspoons minced garlic

¼ teaspoon red pepper flakes

1 large bunch kale, stemmed and torn

Salt

Freshly ground black pepper

1½ cups cooked white beans (cannellini, navy, or great northern) or 1 (15-ounce) can, drained and rinsed

Juice and grated zest of 1 lemon

3 tablespoons toasted pine nuts

1. In a large skillet, warm the oil over medium heat. Add the garlic and red pepper flakes and sauté for 1 minute. Add the kale and season it with salt and pepper. Sauté for about 4 minutes, until the kale is wilted.

2. Add the beans and cook for about 2 minutes, until heated through. Add the lemon juice and zest, stir to combine, and top the dish with the pine nuts. Store this dish in an airtight container in the refrigerator for up to 4 days.

**Tip:** If you enjoy seafood, this is a good recipe to serve with shrimp. To do so, sauté a couple of minced garlic cloves in olive oil over medium heat and cook the shrimp for 3 to 5 minutes, stirring once or twice until cooked through. Squeeze lemon juice over the top and serve alongside the beans and kale.

*Per Serving:* Calories: 111; Total fat: 6g; Protein: 2g; Carbohydrates: 12g; Fiber: 5g

# Potato and Pinto Bean Hash

SERVES 4 TO 6 / PREP TIME: 10 MINUTES / COOK TIME: 15 MINUTES

5 INGREDIENT / GLUTEN-FREE / NUT-FREE / QUICK / SOY-FREE

This easy version of hash begins with seasoned potatoes, adding pinto beans in right at the end. For a different spin, try sweet potatoes in place of the russet.

2 teaspoons extra-virgin olive oil

1 large (about 10 ounces) russet potato, unpeeled and cut into a ¼-inch dice

1 small onion, chopped

1 small red bell pepper, chopped

1 teaspoon ground cumin

1½ cups cooked pinto beans or 1 (15-ounce) can, drained and rinsed

4 cups (about 5 ounces) baby spinach

½ teaspoon salt

¼ teaspoon freshly ground black pepper

1. In a large skillet, heat the olive oil over medium-high heat. Add the potato, onion, bell pepper, and cumin and cook for about 10 minutes, stirring frequently, until the potato cubes are tender.

2. Reduce the heat to medium. Add the beans, spinach, salt, and pepper, stir to combine, and cover. Steam for about 3 minutes, until the spinach begins to lightly wilt. Serve warm.

**Tip:** If you eat meat, add three slices of chopped prosciutto to the hash along with the spinach in step 2 to heat through before serving.

*Per Serving:* Calories: 241; Total fat: 3g; Protein: 11g; Carbohydrates: 44g; Fiber: 10g

# Three-Bean Bonanza

SERVES 4 / PREP TIME: 10 MINUTES

GLUTEN-FREE / NO COOK / NUT-FREE / OIL-FREE / QUICK / SOY-FREE

This classic salad is a perfect quick meal, and when made using canned beans, it is all the easier. It tastes great after marinating for a day or two in the refrigerator, so it's great for easy meal prep for a busy week. The firm texture of chickpeas pairs well with the softer kidney beans and green beans, but any combination of beans you have on hand can shine in this simple combination.

1½ cups cooked chickpeas or 1 (15-ounce) can, drained and rinsed

1½ cups cooked kidney beans or 1 (15-ounce) can, drained and rinsed

1½ cups cooked green beans or 1 (14.5-ounce) can, drained and rinsed

1 small yellow or sweet onion, diced

¼ cup apple cider vinegar

2 tablespoons extra-virgin olive oil (optional)

½ teaspoon red pepper flakes

½ to 1 teaspoon salt

In a large bowl, combine the chickpeas, kidney beans, green beans, onion, vinegar, oil (if using), and red pepper flakes. Season with salt and toss until well mixed and coated. Store in an airtight container in the refrigerator for up to 5 days.

**Tip:** This recipe is versatile. You can switch up the types of beans, use frozen or fresh green beans, or use rice vinegar in place of apple cider vinegar.

*Per Serving:* Calories: 300; Total fat: 3g; Protein: 17g; Carbohydrates: 53g; Fiber: 17g

# White Bean Pesto Salad

SERVES 4 / PREP TIME: 15 MINUTES

GLUTEN-FREE / NO COOK / OIL-FREE / QUICK / SOY-FREE

This is a fresh way to enjoy an anything-but-basic bean salad. We start with a vegan version of pesto (no Parmesan) and simply toss it with beans and greens. Bonus: Use this pesto as a pizza sauce, sandwich spread, salad dressing, or vegetable dip.

**FOR THE PESTO**

3 ounces fresh basil leaves (3 loosely packed cups)

3 ounces arugula (4 loosely packed cups)

½ cup walnuts

3 tablespoons freshly squeezed lemon juice (1 large lemon)

2 tablespoons nutritional yeast

1 tablespoon minced garlic (about 3 cloves)

½ teaspoon salt

¼ teaspoon freshly ground black pepper

1 to 2 teaspoons water or extra-virgin olive oil

**FOR THE SALAD**

16 ounces baby spinach

1½ cups cooked white beans (cannellini, navy, or great northern) or 1 (15-ounce) can, drained and rinsed

1 large yellow bell pepper, cut into thin strips

1 cup cherry tomatoes, halved

1. **MAKE THE PESTO:** In a food processor, combine the basil, arugula, walnuts, lemon juice, nutritional yeast, garlic, salt, and pepper. Pulse until combined, creating a thick texture. Add 1 teaspoon of water and blend. Add more water, as necessary, to create a paste.

2. **MAKE THE SALAD:** In a large bowl, combine the spinach, beans, bell pepper, and tomatoes. Scrape the pesto into the bowl and toss gently to coat. Serve.

**Tip:** The pesto can be prepared up to 5 days in advance; refrigerate in an airtight container.

**Tip:** Pesto pasta is great because it is easily customizable. To add more protein to the pasta, top with 8 ounces sautéed shrimp, chicken breast, or tofu.

*Per Serving:* Calories: 316; Total fat: 12g; Protein: 19g; Carbohydrates: 40g; Fiber: 17g

# Zesty Chickpea, Tomato, and Kalamata Olive Salad

SERVES 4 / PREP TIME: 15 MINUTES

GLUTEN-FREE / NO COOK / NUT-FREE / QUICK / SOY-FREE

Chickpeas are one of my favorite legumes because of their firm texture that works so well in salads. This hearty chickpea salad is easy to make in just minutes and only requires some quick chopping when using canned chickpeas. While this is good fresh, it also makes great leftovers, as the vegetables marinate in the dressing and taste even better a couple of days later. Try serving this as a sandwich or over greens for a twist.

**FOR THE SALAD**

1½ cups cooked chickpeas or 1 (15-ounce) can, drained and rinsed

1 seedless cucumber, peeled and chopped

1 cup cherry or grape tomatoes, halved

½ red bell pepper, finely chopped

½ red onion, sliced into half-moons

¼ cup halved pitted kalamata olives

¼ cup chopped fresh parsley

**FOR THE DRESSING**

3 tablespoons extra-virgin olive oil

2 tablespoons red wine vinegar

1 garlic clove, minced

½ teaspoon salt

¼ teaspoon freshly ground black pepper

1. **MAKE THE SALAD:** In a large bowl, mix together the chickpeas, cucumber, tomatoes, bell pepper, onion, olives, and parsley.
2. **MAKE THE DRESSING:** In a small bowl, whisk together the oil, vinegar, garlic, salt, and pepper. Drizzle over the salad and toss, then serve.

**Tip:** This is also great with 1 tablespoon of crumbled feta sprinkled over top of each serving, if desired.

**Tip:** You can change up the flavor by adding whatever fresh herbs you have on hand: oregano, thyme, and basil all work great in this salad.

*Per Serving:* Calories: 234; Total fat: 13g; Protein: 7g; Carbohydrates: 25g; Fiber: 7g

# Chopped Avocado and Chickpea Salad

SERVES 6 / PREP TIME: 15 MINUTES

GLUTEN-FREE / NO COOK / NUT-FREE / QUICK / SOY-FREE

This is the perfect salad for weekday lunches. The chickpeas give this salad added protein and fiber, and the avocado adds a creaminess that pairs well with the snappy bite from the onion and parsley. If making the salad in advance, wait to add the avocado until you're ready to serve it to prevent browning.

**FOR THE DRESSING**

¼ cup grapeseed or extra-virgin olive oil

3 tablespoons red wine or apple cider vinegar

Juice of ½ lemon

¼ teaspoon salt

¼ teaspoon freshly ground black pepper

**FOR THE SALAD**

1½ cups cooked chickpeas or 1 (15-ounce) can, drained and rinsed

2 seedless cucumbers, diced

1 pint grape tomatoes, halved

1 yellow bell pepper, diced

1 avocado, peeled, pitted, and diced

1 cup sliced black olives

½ cup diced red onion

½ cup chopped fresh parsley

1. **MAKE THE DRESSING:** In a jar with a tight-fitting lid, combine the oil, vinegar, lemon juice, salt, and pepper. Cover tightly and shake to combine.

2. **MAKE THE SALAD:** In a large bowl, combine the chickpeas, cucumbers, tomatoes, bell pepper, avocado, olives, onion, and parsley. Add the dressing, toss to combine, and serve.

*Per Serving:* Calories: 247; Total fat: 17g; Protein: 6g; Carbohydrates: 22g; Fiber: 7g

# Gigante Bean, Sun-Dried Tomato, and Olive Salad

SERVES 6 / PREP TIME: 10 MINUTES

5 INGREDIENT / GLUTEN-FREE / NO COOK / NUT-FREE / QUICK / SOY-FREE

Gigante beans are perfect for a marinated salad like this because they are firm and hold their shape while taking on the flavors of the dish. Serve this as a side or over brown rice or quinoa to make it a meal. Like many marinated salads, this one tastes even better after a day of marinating in the refrigerator, so feel free to make this in advance of serving.

**3 cups cooked gigante beans**

**½ cup halved pitted kalamata olives**

**¼ cup thinly sliced sun-dried tomatoes**

**2 tablespoons chopped fresh parsley**

**2 tablespoons red wine vinegar**

**2 tablespoons extra-virgin olive oil**

**Freshly ground black pepper**

In a medium bowl, toss together the beans, olives, sun-dried tomatoes, and parsley. In a small bowl, whisk the vinegar and olive oil. Season with pepper. Pour the dressing into the beans and vegetables and toss to combine. Serve immediately or chill before serving.

**Tip:** Like chickpeas, gigante beans are a great salad bean and can be mixed with any number of flavors. Try making a salad with the beans, celery, bell peppers, tomatoes, scallions, and an Italian vinaigrette for a different take on a gigante salad.

*Per Serving:* Calories: 169; Total fat: 7g; Protein: 6g; Carbohydrates: 22g; Fiber: 8g

# Warm Fava Bean and Hearts of Palm Salad

SERVES 4 / PREP TIME: 10 MINUTES / COOK TIME: 10 MINUTES

GLUTEN-FREE / NUT-FREE / QUICK / SOY-FREE

This simple sautéed meal is inspired by one of the healthiest cuisines in the world: Mediterranean. You can also use butter beans or any other white bean and replace the hearts of palm with artichoke hearts. Serve in a bowl with a hearty grain, such as farro or pearl barley, or over a bed of raw arugula, which will wilt slightly under the weight of the warm beans, for a complete meal.

**1 teaspoon extra-virgin olive oil**

**1 small onion, diced**

**2 teaspoons minced garlic (about 2 cloves)**

**1½ cups cooked fava beans or 1 (15-ounce) can fava beans, drained and rinsed**

**1 teaspoon dried basil**

**½ teaspoon ground cumin**

**¼ cup white wine vinegar**

**1 (14-ounce) can hearts of palm, drained and sliced into ¼-inch rounds**

1. In a large skillet, heat the oil over medium-high heat. Add the onion and garlic and sauté for about 3 minutes, until softened. Add the beans, basil, cumin, and vinegar. Stir to combine well. Cover, reduce the heat to low, and simmer for 5 minutes.

2. Uncover, increase the heat to medium, and add the hearts of palm. Gently toss together and cook for 2 minutes, long enough to warm up the hearts of palm; then serve.

*Per Serving:* Calories: 106; Total fat: 2g; Protein: 7g; Carbohydrates: 17g; Fiber: 5g

# White Bean Salad with Tahini Dressing

**SERVES 6 / PREP TIME: 15 MINUTES**

GLUTEN-FREE / NO COOK / NUT-FREE / QUICK / SOY-FREE

A garlicky lemon-tahini sauce perfectly complements mild white beans, and pumpkin seeds add the perfect crunch.

2 tablespoons extra-virgin olive oil

2 tablespoons tahini

2 tablespoons freshly squeezed lemon juice

1 teaspoon minced garlic

Salt

Freshly ground black pepper

3 cups cooked white beans (cannellini, navy, or great northern) or 2 (15-ounce) cans, drained and rinsed

1 red bell pepper, diced

½ cup shredded carrots

½ cup diced celery

2 tablespoons chopped fresh parsley

½ cup salted pumpkin seeds

1. In a small bowl, whisk together the oil, tahini, lemon juice, and garlic. Season the dressing with salt and pepper.

2. In a large bowl, combine the beans, bell pepper, carrots, celery, and parsley. Toss with the dressing and top with the pumpkin seeds; then serve.

**Tip:** Store this salad in an airtight container in the refrigerator for up to 4 days.

*Per Serving:* Calories: 255; Total fat: 13g; Protein: 11g; Carbohydrates: 25g; Fiber: 8g

# Black Bean Taco Salad

SERVES 4 / PREP TIME: 15 MINUTES / COOK TIME: 15 MINUTES

GLUTEN-FREE / NUT-FREE / QUICK

Taco salad is really easy to make and a super hearty main course salad. Make the crispy tortilla shreds in the oven while you make the salad, or try making tortilla bowls instead of chips: Lightly coat the tortillas with cooking spray and nestle them over the cups of an upside-down muffin tin to form bowls. Bake at 375°F for about 15 minutes, until crisp.

**FOR THE SALAD**

Olive oil cooking spray

4 (6-inch) corn tortillas

1 small head romaine lettuce, chopped (about 4 cups)

1½ cups cooked black beans or 1 (15-ounce) can, drained and rinsed

1 (15-ounce) can corn, drained

½ red bell pepper, finely chopped

¼ cup chopped red onion

2 tablespoons chopped fresh cilantro

**FOR THE DRESSING**

½ cup Plant-Based Sour Cream (page 93) or store-bought

¼ cup salsa

½ teaspoon ground cumin

1. Preheat the oven to 350°F. Spray a baking sheet with cooking spray.

2. **MAKE THE SALAD:** On a clean work surface, stack the tortillas and cut in half. Stack the two halves on top of each other and cut the tortillas into ½-inch strips.

3. Arrange the tortilla strips in a single layer on the prepared baking sheet. Spray lightly with cooking spray. Bake for about 15 minutes, flipping halfway through, until lightly browned. The pieces will further crisp after you remove them from the oven, so you don't have to wait until they are crunchy in the oven.

4. In a large bowl, toss the lettuce, beans, corn, bell pepper, onion, and cilantro.

5. **MAKE THE DRESSING:** In a food processor, combine the sour cream, salsa, and cumin. Add water, 2 tablespoons at a time, to thin the dressing.

6. Toss the dressing with the salad and serve.

---

Tip: You can brown 8 ounces of ground turkey or beef, season it with 1 teaspoon each of chili powder, onion powder, and garlic powder and ½ teaspoon of ground cumin, and add it to the salad as a whole or in individual servings.

*Per Serving:* Calories: 251; Total fat: 7g; Protein: 10g; Carbohydrates: 43g; Fiber: 12g

CHAPTER FOUR

# SOUPS AND STEWS

< Tex-Mex Quinoa Vegetable Soup, page 54

# Navy Bean and Veggie Soup

SERVES 4 / PREP TIME: 10 MINUTES / COOK TIME: 25 MINUTES

FREEZABLE / GLUTEN-FREE / NUT-FREE / SOY-FREE

This simple veggie soup features a rainbow of colors, creamy navy beans, and brown rice to create a hearty dish that comes together in minutes. Use this recipe as a blueprint and add seasonal vegetables to make it your own.

2 tablespoons extra-virgin olive oil

1 onion, chopped

3 garlic cloves, minced

4 cups Everyday Vegetable Broth (page 92) or store-bought low-sodium broth

1½ cups cooked navy beans or 1 (15-ounce) can navy beans, drained and rinsed

1 (15-ounce) can diced tomatoes, drained

¾ cup chopped carrots

2 celery stalks, chopped

2 tablespoons chopped fresh parsley

2 teaspoons fresh thyme leaves

½ teaspoon salt

1 zucchini, chopped

1 cup cooked brown rice

1. In a large pot, heat the oil over medium-high heat. Add the onion and sauté for 3 to 5 minutes, until softened. Add the garlic and cook for about 30 seconds, until fragrant.

2. Add the broth, beans, tomatoes, carrots, celery, parsley, thyme, and salt. Bring to a boil; then reduce the heat to low. Simmer for about 10 minutes, until the vegetables are tender. Add the zucchini and rice and cook for about 5 minutes more, until heated through and the zucchini is tender. Serve.

**Tip:** This soup is seasoned with fresh parsley and thyme, but other seasonings, like Italian seasoning, fresh basil, or rosemary, are nice additions to change up the flavor profile.

*Per Serving:* Calories: 321; Total fat: 8g; Protein: 11g; Carbohydrates: 52g; Fiber: 14g

# Spicy Black Bean Soup

SERVES 6 / PREP TIME: 10 MINUTES / COOK TIME: 25 MINUTES

FREEZABLE / GLUTEN-FREE / NUT-FREE / SOY-FREE

Black bean soup is a winter favorite in my house. I like to serve it with corn bread and a green salad, but garnishes like avocado and tortilla chips are also welcome additions to this simple soup. To control the amount of heat in your dish, start with only half of the jalapeño pepper and taste before adding the whole thing.

2 tablespoons extra-virgin olive oil

1 large onion, chopped

2 celery stalks, chopped

1 carrot, chopped

1 jalapeño pepper, seeded and coarsely chopped

3 garlic cloves, minced

1 tablespoon ground cumin

4½ cups cooked black beans or 3 (15-ounce) cans, drained and rinsed

4 cups Everyday Vegetable Broth (page 92) or store-bought low-sodium broth

Salt

Freshly ground black pepper

Juice of 1 lime

¼ cup chopped fresh cilantro, for garnish

Plant-Based Sour Cream (page 93) or store-bought, for topping (optional)

1. In a large pot, heat the oil over medium-high heat. Add the onion, celery, carrot, and jalapeño and cook for 5 to 6 minutes, stirring regularly, until starting to soften. Add the garlic and cumin and stir for about 30 seconds, until just fragrant.

2. Add the beans and broth and bring to a boil; then reduce the heat to low. Simmer for about 15 minutes, until the flavors meld.

3. Using an immersion blender or a stand blender working in batches, puree the soup. Season with salt and pepper and add the lime juice. Serve topped with the cilantro and sour cream (if using).

**Tip:** Black beans contain more antioxidants than any other beans due to their rich color. Rich in anthocyanins, a group of flavonoids that create the dark purple and red colors in foods, black beans are a phytonutrient powerhouse.

*Per Serving:* Calories: 261; Total fat: 6g; Protein: 14g; Carbohydrates: 41g; Fiber: 14g

# Cranberry Bean Minestrone Soup

SERVES 6 / PREP TIME: 15 MINUTES / COOK TIME: 35 MINUTES

FREEZABLE / NUT-FREE / SOY-FREE

This veggie-rich minestrone soup is loaded with flavor and so easy to make. It's really quick to put together if you have cooked cranberry beans prepared, but if not, you can also make this in the slow cooker by combining soaked beans, all of the other ingredients, and 2 more cups of water, and cooking for 6 to 8 hours on low.

2 tablespoons extra-virgin olive oil

1 onion, chopped

1 carrot, chopped

2 celery stalks, chopped

2 garlic cloves, minced

6 cups Everyday Vegetable Broth (page 92) or store-bought low-sodium broth

1 (28-ounce) can whole tomatoes, drained

1½ cups cooked cranberry beans or 1 (15-ounce) can, drained and rinsed

1 teaspoon Italian seasoning

1 teaspoon salt

¼ teaspoon freshly ground black pepper

1 zucchini, chopped

1 cup whole-grain small shell pasta

1 cup chopped fresh or frozen spinach

1 cup fresh or frozen peas

1. In a large pot, heat the oil over medium-high heat. Add the onion, carrot, and celery and sauté for about 5 minutes, until softened. Add the garlic and cook for about 30 seconds, until fragrant.

2. Add the broth, tomatoes, beans, Italian seasoning, salt, and pepper. Bring to a boil; then reduce the heat to low. Simmer for about 15 minutes, until the flavors meld. Add the zucchini and pasta and simmer for about 5 minutes, until the pasta is nearly softened.

3. Add the spinach and peas and cook for about 5 more minutes, until the zucchini is tender and the noodles are soft. Season with additional salt, if needed, and serve.

**Tip:** This is a soup that is customizable to whatever vegetables you have on hand based on the season. Replace the spinach with any other tender greens you have available—like chard, kale, or young collard, mustard, or turnip greens—and the zucchini with other summer squash.

*Per Serving:* Calories: 285; Total fat: 6g; Protein: 13g; Carbohydrates: 48g; Fiber: 12g

## Chickpea Noodle Soup

SERVES 6 / PREP TIME: 15 MINUTES / COOK TIME: 25 MINUTES

NUT-FREE / SOY-FREE

Chicken noodle soup is a comfort food classic, and this plant-based version is reimagined using chickpeas as the protein source with equally comforting results. Use any noodles you want, but my favorites are smaller varieties, like elbow or farfalle, so you can enjoy noodles with nearly every bite.

1 tablespoon extra-virgin olive oil

1 small onion, chopped

4 carrots, chopped

4 celery stalks, chopped

2 garlic cloves, minced

8 cups Everyday Vegetable Broth (page 92) or store-bought low-sodium broth

6 ounces whole-grain pasta of choice

1½ cups cooked chickpeas or 1 (15-ounce) can, drained and rinsed

½ teaspoon dried basil

½ teaspoon dried oregano

½ teaspoon dried thyme

½ teaspoon dried sage

Salt

Freshly ground black pepper

1. In a large stockpot over medium-high heat, heat the oil. Add the onion and cook for about 5 minutes, stirring occasionally, until softened. Add the carrots, celery, and garlic. Cook for about 5 minutes more, until the vegetables soften.

2. Add the broth, pasta, chickpeas, basil, oregano, thyme, and sage. Bring to a boil; then reduce the heat to low. Simmer for 10 to 12 minutes, stirring frequently, until the pasta is tender. Remove from the heat. Taste and season with salt and pepper; then serve.

**Tip:** If you have poultry seasoning on hand, use 2 teaspoons of it instead of the dried herbs. Poultry seasoning doesn't actually contain any chicken—it's a blend of herbs and spices typically used to season poultry and is safe for vegans.

*Per Serving:* Calories: 240; Total fat: 4g; Protein: 9g; Carbohydrates: 44g; Fiber: 7g

# Tex-Mex Quinoa Vegetable Soup

SERVES 6 / PREP TIME: 20 MINUTES / COOK TIME: 1 HOUR 10 MINUTES

FREEZABLE / GLUTEN-FREE / NUT-FREE / OIL-FREE / SOY-FREE

The flavors of this soup come from the natural sweetness of corn, carrots, and tomatoes, balanced with beans and nutty-tasting quinoa. Serve this soup with a generous portion of chopped avocado, a squeeze of fresh lime juice, and a sprinkle of fresh cilantro.

1 cup quinoa

½ large onion, diced

2 carrots, cut into coins

2 celery stalks, sliced

2 garlic cloves, minced

1 tablespoon water, plus more as needed

¼ cup tomato paste

6 cups Everyday Vegetable Broth (page 92) or store-bought low-sodium broth, plus more as needed

1 zucchini, cut into coins and quartered

1 (14-ounce) can corn, drained

1 (14-ounce) can diced tomatoes

1½ cups cooked black beans or 1 (15-ounce) can, drained and rinsed

1½ cups cooked kidney beans or 1 (15-ounce) can, drained and rinsed

2 teaspoons chili powder

1 teaspoon ground cumin

1 teaspoon salt

1. Place the quinoa in a fine-mesh sieve and rinse under cold water for 2 to 3 minutes, or until the cloudy water becomes clear.

2. In a large pot, combine the onion, carrots, celery, garlic, and water. Cook for 2 to 3 minutes. Stir in the tomato paste to combine.

3. Add the broth, zucchini, corn, tomatoes and their juices, black beans, kidney beans, chili powder, cumin, and salt. Stir well. The tomato paste will fully incorporate as the soup cooks.

4. Turn the heat to medium-low. Cover the pot and cook for 45 to 60 minutes, stirring occasionally to prevent the tomatoes from settling to the bottom and scorching. If the soup seems too thick, add more broth or water, ½ cup at a time, until your desired consistency is met. Serve.

**Tip:** Black beans and kidney beans are the most common types used for Tex-Mex cuisine, but use any variety you prefer. This recipe is also delicious with jalapeño peppers or other hot peppers.

*Per Serving:* Calories: 334; Total fat: 4g; Protein: 16g; Carbohydrates: 62g; Fiber: 14g

# Creamy Fava Bean and Mint Soup

SERVES 4 / PREP TIME: 15 MINUTES / COOK TIME: 45 MINUTES

5 INGREDIENT / GLUTEN-FREE / NUT-FREE / SOY-FREE

This is a really nice soup to have in early spring, when fava beans are available fresh at markets. While it is a labor of love to remove the pods' shells and then each individual shell of the fava beans, it helps yield an extra-creamy result in the finished product.

2 tablespoons extra-virgin olive oil

1 large onion, chopped

1 large russet potato, peeled and chopped

3 cups shelled fresh or thawed frozen fava beans

4 cups Everyday Vegetable Broth (page 92) or store-bought low-sodium broth

¼ teaspoon salt

3 tablespoons finely chopped fresh mint, plus more for garnish

1. In a large pot, heat the oil over medium heat. Add the onion and sauté for about 5 minutes, until softened.

2. Add the potato and cook, stirring, for about 5 more minutes. Add the beans, broth, and salt. Bring to a boil; then reduce the heat to low. Cover and simmer for 25 to 30 minutes, until the beans and potatoes are tender.

3. Using an immersion blender or working in batches using a stand blender, puree the soup. Stir in the mint and mix well. Season with additional salt as needed. Serve warm, garnished with additional mint.

**Tip:** If you can't find green fava beans, frozen green peas can be used in their place for a similar soup.

*Per Serving:* Calories: 271; Total fat: 8g; Protein: 11g; Carbohydrates: 42g; Fiber: 9g

# Curried Mung Bean and Chard Soup

SERVES 6 / PREP TIME: 10 MINUTES / COOK TIME: 50 MINUTES

FREEZABLE / GLUTEN-FREE / SOY-FREE

Mung beans hold their shape a bit better than brown lentils, but in this soup, they melt to form a savory creamy base. Coconut milk is added at the end and really turns the flavor up a notch. You can substitute light coconut milk if you must, but full fat makes it all the more delicious.

2 tablespoons extra-virgin olive oil

1 large onion, chopped

2 celery stalks, chopped

1 carrot, chopped

3 garlic cloves, minced

1 tablespoon curry powder

1 teaspoon ground turmeric

4 cups Everyday Vegetable Broth (page 92) or store-bought low-sodium broth

2 cups water

1 cup dried mung beans

1 bunch Swiss or rainbow chard, chopped

1 tomato, chopped

1 cup canned full-fat coconut milk

1 teaspoon salt

1. In a large pot, heat the oil over medium-high heat. Add the onion, celery, and carrot and sauté for about 5 minutes, until softened.

2. Stir in the garlic, curry powder, and turmeric and stir for about 30 seconds, until mixed well and fragrant. Add the broth, water, and beans. Bring to a boil; then reduce the heat to low. Simmer for about 30 minutes, stirring occasionally, until the beans are tender.

3. Add the chard, tomato, and coconut milk and continue to cook for about 10 minutes, until the flavors meld. Season with the salt and serve.

**Tip:** Chard's thick stems hold up nicely in this soup for a good textural balance, making it an ideal choice, but other mild-flavored greens like spinach and other baby greens can be used in its place. Reduce cooking time to just a couple minutes after you add the spinach, until just wilted.

*Per Serving:* Calories: 279; Total fat: 12g; Protein: 11g; Carbohydrates: 34g; Fiber: 9g

# Creamy Cauliflower and White Bean Soup with Herbed Croutons

SERVES 4 / PREP TIME: 10 MINUTES / COOK TIME: 25 MINUTES

NUT-FREE / SOY-FREE

The white beans and cauliflower in this soup form a creamy base and lovely flavor, especially when paired with the crunchy homemade croutons used as garnish. This simple stovetop version is quick and requires just one dish, but for a little extra work, you can roast the cauliflower instead of boiling it to add even more flavor, if desired.

3 tablespoons extra-virgin olive oil, divided

1 onion, chopped

1 celery stalk, chopped

3 garlic cloves, chopped

1 cauliflower head, broken into florets

4 cups Everyday Vegetable Broth (page 92) or store-bought low-sodium broth

1½ cups cooked white beans (cannellini, navy, or great northern) or 1 (15-ounce) can, drained and rinsed

½ teaspoon salt

Freshly ground black pepper

2 slices whole-grain sourdough or other crusty bread, cut into cubes

½ teaspoon dried thyme

1. Preheat the oven to 400°F.
2. In a large pot, heat 2 tablespoons of oil over medium-high heat. Add the onion and celery and cook for 3 to 5 minutes, until softened. Add the garlic and cook for about 30 seconds, until fragrant. Add the cauliflower, broth, and beans. Bring to a boil; then reduce the heat to medium-low. Simmer for about 15 minutes, until the cauliflower is tender.
3. While the soup is simmering, spread the bread in a single layer on a baking sheet and toast for 10 to 15 minutes, until golden brown and crisp.
4. Using an immersion blender or working in batches using a stand blender, puree the soup. Season with the salt and pepper to taste.
5. In a medium bowl, toss the croutons with the remaining 1 tablespoon of oil and the thyme. Serve the soup topped with the croutons.

**Tip:** To make the soup even creamier, add ¼ cup of heavy cream or whole milk to the soup at the end of step 4 and heat through.

*Per Serving:* Calories: 297; Total fat: 11g; Protein: 11g; Carbohydrates: 39g; Fiber: 10g

# Miso, Lentil, and Kale Soup

SERVES 4 / PREP TIME: 15 MINUTES / COOK TIME: 35 MINUTES

FREEZABLE / GLUTEN-FREE / NUT-FREE / OIL-FREE

Lentils are high in fiber, iron, protein, and a broad range of phytochemicals that protect against type 2 diabetes and heart disease. The most common lentil, the brown lentil, retains its shape during cooking and gives an earthy flavor to dishes. This recipe also uses miso, various root vegetables, and kale to create a nutritious dish full of umami flavor.

**4 large carrots, thinly sliced**

**4 celery stalks, thinly sliced**

**2 small shallots, diced**

**2 garlic cloves, minced**

**1 tablespoon water, plus more as needed**

**3 cups baby potatoes, unpeeled, halved, and quartered**

**4 cups Everyday Vegetable Broth (page 92) or store-bought low-sodium broth**

**1 cup dried brown lentils, rinsed**

**1 tablespoon red miso paste**

**3 thyme sprigs**

**½ teaspoon salt**

**¼ teaspoon freshly ground black pepper**

**2 cups coarsely chopped kale**

1. In a large pot over medium-high heat, combine the carrots, celery, shallots, garlic, and water. Cook for 1 to 2 minutes, adding water 1 tablespoon at a time as needed to prevent burning, until the shallots and celery are translucent. Add the potatoes and cook for 3 to 4 minutes.

2. Add the broth; then add the lentils, miso paste, thyme, salt, and pepper. Bring the soup to a simmer. Cover and cook for 15 to 20 minutes, or until the lentils and potatoes are tender. Add the kale and cook for 3 to 4 minutes, until wilted.

3. Serve warm. Refrigerate leftovers in an airtight container for up to 1 week or freeze for 4 to 6 months. The lentils will absorb some of the liquid; add more liquid or enjoy a thicker soup.

**Tip:** The shallots can be replaced with 1 onion, but shallots are less acidic and bring a slight sweetness.

*Per Serving:* Calories: 292; Total fat: 2g; Protein: 15g; Carbohydrates: 58g; Fiber: 12g

# Lemony Split Pea Soup

SERVES 8 / PREP TIME: 5 MINUTES / COOK TIME: 30 MINUTES

GLUTEN-FREE / OIL-FREE / SOY-FREE

Pea soup is a warming winter soup that is super easy and economical to make. Because split peas are quick cooking, it's a perfect weeknight soup, too. If you can't find yellow split peas, green split peas work just as well.

6 cups Everyday Vegetable Broth (page 92) or store-bought low-sodium broth

1½ cups dried yellow split peas

2 cups sliced carrots

1 cup frozen corn

2 teaspoons ground cumin

1 teaspoon onion powder

1 teaspoon garlic powder

1 teaspoon curry powder

⅛ teaspoon ground turmeric

⅛ teaspoon ground cayenne pepper

¼ cup canned full-fat coconut milk

Juice and grated zest of 1 lemon

Salt

Freshly ground black pepper

1. In a large pot, combine the broth, split peas, carrots, corn, cumin, onion powder, garlic powder, curry powder, turmeric, and cayenne. Stir well. Bring to a boil; then reduce the heat to medium. Simmer for 25 minutes, until the split peas are tender.

2. Remove from the heat and stir in the coconut milk and lemon juice and zest. Season with salt and pepper and serve.

**Tip:** To give this soup a creamier texture, use an immersion blender to puree the soup (adding a little extra coconut milk to loosen if needed), or working in small batches, blend it in a stand blender.

*Per Serving:* Calories: 179; Total fat: 3g; Protein: 9g; Carbohydrates: 31g; Fiber: 10g

# Spiced Carrot-Lentil Soup

SERVES 4 / PREP TIME: 10 MINUTES / COOK TIME: 35 MINUTES

GLUTEN-FREE / SOY-FREE

The carrot, tomatoes, and red lentils used in this dish create a vibrant, rich orange hue. The lentils make it a really light yet filling soup. It's perfect as a side to a light wrap or sandwich. The combination of warming cumin, coriander, and turmeric perfectly spices the soup, and the coconut milk makes it luxuriously creamy.

**4 cups Everyday Vegetable Broth (page 92) or store-bought low-sodium broth**

**3 large carrots, chopped**

**1 (15-ounce) can diced tomatoes, drained**

**½ cup dried red lentils, rinsed**

**1 onion, chopped**

**1 tablespoon extra-virgin olive oil**

**1 teaspoon ground cumin**

**1 teaspoon ground coriander**

**½ teaspoon ground turmeric**

**Juice from ½ lemon**

**½ teaspoon salt**

**1 cup canned full-fat coconut milk**

**1 cup water**

1. In a large pot over high heat, combine the broth, carrots, tomatoes, lentils, and onion. Bring to a boil; then reduce the heat to medium-low. Cover and cook for about 20 minutes, until the carrots and lentils are tender.

2. While the soup is cooking, in a small skillet, heat the oil over medium-low heat. Add the cumin, coriander, and turmeric and stir for about 30 seconds, until fragrant. Add the lemon juice and salt and remove from the heat.

3. Using an immersion blender or working in batches using a stand blender, puree the soup. Add the spice mixture and coconut milk and stir. Add the water and bring to a simmer. Cook for about 10 minutes, until the flavors meld. Serve.

**Tip:** If you don't have red lentils, brown or green lentils can be used in their place, but the color won't be the same.

*Per Serving:* Calories: 317; Total fat: 15g; Protein: 10g; Carbohydrates: 39g; Fiber: 8g

# White Bean, Potato, and Leek Soup

SERVES 6 / PREP TIME: 15 MINUTES / COOK TIME: 30 MINUTES

5 INGREDIENT / GLUTEN-FREE / NUT-FREE / SOY-FREE

White beans and buttery Yukon Gold potatoes combine to make a luxurious base in this easy weeknight meal. Leeks provide a nice alternative to onions for flavoring in this creamy soup.

2 tablespoons extra-virgin olive oil

2 leeks, rinsed well and chopped

3 garlic cloves, minced

4 cups Everyday Vegetable Broth (page 92) or store-bought low-sodium broth

2 large Yukon Gold potatoes, peeled and chopped

1½ cups cooked white beans (cannellini, navy, or great northern) or 1 (15-ounce) can, drained and rinsed

½ teaspoon salt

¼ teaspoon freshly ground black pepper

1. In a large pot, heat the oil over medium-high heat. Add the leeks and cook for about 5 minutes, until softened. Add the garlic and cook for about 30 seconds, until fragrant.

2. Add the broth and potatoes and bring to a boil; then reduce the heat to low. Cover and simmer for about 15 minutes, until the potatoes are fork-tender. Add the beans, salt, and pepper and simmer for 2 to 3 minutes, until heated through. Using an immersion blender or working in batches using a stand blender, puree the soup. Serve.

**Tip:** Leeks tend to have dirt stuck in between their layers, so be sure to wash them thoroughly or you'll end up with a grainy soup. Soaking the leeks, halved lengthwise, in water, is the easiest way to remove the dirt.

**Tip:** Sprinkle 1 or 2 tablespoons of bacon or vegan bacon over the soup to serve.

*Per Serving:* Calories: 231; Total fat: 5g; Protein: 8g; Carbohydrates: 40g; Fiber: 8g

# Spicy Butternut Squash and Adzuki Bean Soup

SERVES 6 / PREP TIME: 10 MINUTES / COOK TIME: 30 MINUTES
FREEZABLE / GLUTEN-FREE / NUT-FREE / SOY-FREE

With its rich, creamy flesh, butternut squash is one of my favorites for soup. To make the squash easier to peel, poke a hole in it with a knife and microwave for 2 to 3 minutes until just slightly softer; then use a vegetable peeler to remove its skin with ease. Some grocery stores also sell cut squash that can be used here to reduce prep time.

2 tablespoons extra-virgin olive oil

1 large onion, chopped

3 garlic cloves, minced

1 tablespoon sriracha

6 cups Everyday Vegetable Broth (page 92) or store-bought low-sodium broth

3 cups cooked adzuki beans or 2 (15-ounce) cans, drained and rinsed

2 cups chopped butternut squash

1 (15-ounce) can chopped tomatoes, drained

2 cups chopped fresh or frozen spinach

½ teaspoon salt

1. In a large pot, heat the oil over medium heat. Add the onion and sauté for 3 to 5 minutes, until softened. Add the garlic and cook for about 30 seconds, until fragrant.

2. Add the sriracha and stir to combine. Add the broth, beans, squash, and tomatoes. Bring to a boil; then reduce the heat to medium-low. Simmer for about 15 minutes, until the squash is tender.

3. Add the spinach and stir for 1 to 2 minutes, until wilted. Season with salt and serve.

**Tip:** Any type of winter squash can be used here. Kabocha, a Japanese squash, is also really nice in this soup and doesn't require peeling. Delicata, pumpkin, buttercup, and calabaza work great, too.

*Per Serving:* Calories: 286; Total fat: 5g; Protein: 13g; Carbohydrates: 50g; Fiber: 14g

# Smoky Chickpea Stew

SERVES 4 / PREP TIME: 20 MINUTES / COOK TIME: 30 MINUTES

GLUTEN-FREE / NUT-FREE / OIL-FREE / SOY-FREE

This stew's flavor is less about the ingredients and more about the cooking process. By slowly browning the onions and garlic and cooking the spices, a deep, rich flavor emerges. Serve with crusty whole wheat bread for dipping or a scoop of couscous. Enjoy this stew as is or top as desired. I like coarsely chopped cilantro, scallion greens, and jalapeño pepper.

1 tablespoon Hungarian paprika

1 teaspoon smoked paprika

1 teaspoon ground cumin

1 teaspoon onion powder

1 large onion, coarsely chopped

4 garlic cloves, diced

1 tablespoon water, plus more as needed

2 carrots, diced

1 tablespoon pure maple syrup

1 (28-ounce) can crushed tomatoes

½ cup packed chopped fresh cilantro

1½ cups cooked chickpeas or 1 (15-ounce) can, drained and rinsed

1½ cups cooked kidney beans or 1 (15-ounce) can, drained and rinsed

½ teaspoon salt

Juice of ½ lime

1. In a small bowl, stir together the Hungarian paprika, smoked paprika, cumin, and onion powder. Set aside.

2. In an 8-quart pot, combine the onion, garlic, and 1 tablespoon of water over high heat. Turn the heat to medium-low. Cook for at least 10 minutes, stirring occasionally. Add more water, 1 tablespoon at a time, to prevent burning, until the onion is deeply browned. Stir in the carrots. Turn the heat to high. Stir in the paprika mixture and cook for 30 seconds, stirring continuously to prevent burning. Pour in the maple syrup and cook for 30 seconds more, stirring.

3. Carefully pour in the tomatoes with their juices. To avoid splatter, pour the tomatoes onto a spoon and not directly into the hot pot. Bring to a simmer, stirring; then turn the heat to low. Cover and cook for 10 minutes.

4. Stir in the cilantro, chickpeas, and beans. Cover the pot and cook for 5 minutes more to warm. Season with the salt and sprinkle with the lime juice before serving.

**Tip:** Cooking your spices for 15 to 30 seconds before adding the liquids can bring out their complex flavors. The key to avoiding scorching is to stir continuously and have your liquid ready to add immediately to stop the cooking process.

*Per Serving Calories:* 331; Total fat: 3g; Protein: 17g; Carbohydrates: 65g; Fiber: 15g

# Gigante Bean Stew

SERVES 4 / PREP TIME: 10 MINUTES / COOK TIME: 1 HOUR 10 MINUTES

FREEZABLE / GLUTEN-FREE / NUT-FREE / SOY-FREE

This is a version of *gigantes plaki*, or "Greek baked beans," a popular gigante bean dish in Greece. This recipe cooks down into a thick stew that is great served with crusty bread to sop up the juices. While the cook time is a little longer on this recipe than many of the others in this book, most of it is hands-off time, and the end result is worth the wait.

2 tablespoons extra-virgin olive oil

1 large onion, chopped

3 garlic cloves, minced

3 cups cooked gigante beans

1 (15-ounce) can diced tomatoes, drained

½ cup Everyday Vegetable Broth (page 92) or store-bought low-sodium broth

4 sprigs thyme, leaves removed

1 teaspoon dried oregano

½ teaspoon salt

¼ teaspoon freshly ground black pepper

1. Preheat the oven to 350°F.
2. In a large oven-safe skillet, heat the oil over medium-high heat. Add the onion and cook for about 5 minutes, until softened. Add the garlic and cook for about 30 seconds, until fragrant.
3. Stir in the beans, tomatoes, broth, thyme, oregano, salt, and pepper. Bring to a simmer; then remove from the heat. Cover and transfer to the oven to cook for 50 to 60 minutes, until the sauce thickens. Serve.

**Tip:** Gigante beans are a large, flat, white bean popular in the Mediterranean. If you can't find them near you, they're available online, or you can substitute another white bean in their place.

*Per Serving:* Calories: 332; Total fat: 7g; Protein: 16g; Carbohydrates: 52g; Fiber: 12g

# Three-Bean Chipotle Chili

SERVES 8 / PREP TIME: 10 MINUTES / COOK TIME: 20 MINUTES

FREEZABLE / GLUTEN-FREE / NUT-FREE / QUICK / SOY-FREE

This version of chili turns up the heat a bit with the addition of a smoky chipotle chile in adobo sauce. Using canned beans and with very little prep work, you can have this chili in the pot and simmering within minutes. Corn bread always pairs nicely with chili.

1 (28-ounce) can whole tomatoes

1½ cups cooked kidney beans or 1 (15-ounce) can, drained and rinsed

1½ cups cooked black beans or 1 (15-ounce) can, drained and rinsed

1½ cups cooked white beans (cannellini, navy, or great northern) or 1 (15-ounce) can, drained and rinsed

1 onion, chopped

1 chipotle chile in adobo sauce, chopped

1 teaspoon garlic powder

½ teaspoon salt

Plant-Based Sour Cream (page 93) or store-bought, for serving (optional)

¼ cup chopped scallions, green part only, for serving

Lime wedges, for serving

1. In a large pot over medium heat, combine the tomatoes and their juices, kidney beans, black beans, white beans, onion, chipotle, garlic powder, and salt. Bring to a simmer; then cook, stirring occasionally, for about 15 minutes, until the flavors meld.

2. Serve warm topped with sour cream (if using) and scallions. Serve with the lime wedges for squeezing.

**Tip:** To make this chili with meat, cook 8 ounces of ground turkey in a skillet over medium heat for about 6 minutes, until cooked through. When done, remove any chili being served to vegan guests; then stir in the ground turkey, cook for a few minutes until the flavors meld, and serve.

*Per Serving:* Calories: 164; Total fat: 1g; Protein: 10g; Carbohydrates: 30g; Fiber: 10g

## CHAPTER FIVE

# BEAN SUPPERS

< Roasted Kabocha Squash with Chickpeas, page 72

# Swiss Chard and Black-Eyed Pea Pilaf

SERVES 4 / PREP TIME: 20 MINUTES / COOK TIME: 50 MINUTES

NUT-FREE / SOY-FREE

Swiss chard is a nutrient powerhouse high in antioxidants, iron, fiber, and vitamins A, C, and K. It grows really well in my garden, and I often have more than we can use at one time, so I chop it, blanch it, and freeze it in small bags to save for future use. I highly recommend you do the same; that way, in winter, you can use it in soups and stews—and to make this healthy dish.

**10 cups water, divided**

**1 pound Swiss chard or kale, chopped**

**¼ cup extra-virgin olive oil**

**1 onion, chopped**

**1½ cups cooked black-eyed peas or 1 (15-ounce) can, drained and rinsed**

**1 garlic clove, mashed**

**½ teaspoon ground coriander**

**½ teaspoon salt**

**1 cup coarse bulgur #3**

1.  In a large pot, bring 8 cups of water to a boil over medium heat. Add the chard and return it to a boil. Cook for 5 minutes. Remove from the heat, drain the chard, and set aside to cool.

2.  Return the pot to medium heat and warm the oil. Add the onion and cook for 5 minutes, until softened.

3.  Add the black-eyed peas and cook for 10 minutes more. Stir in the garlic, coriander, salt, and chard. Cook for 1 minute. Pour the remaining 2 cups of water over the vegetables, increase the heat to high, and bring the mixture to a boil.

4.  Add the bulgur and return to a boil; then reduce the heat to medium-low. Cover and cook for 10 minutes. Remove from the heat and let the pilaf rest for 10 minutes before serving.

*Per Serving:* Calories: 307; Total fat: 14g; Protein: 10g; Carbohydrates: 42g; Fiber: 11g

# Tofu, Edamame, and Shiitake Stir-Fry with Rice

This stir-fry is loaded with protein and features the soybean in two forms: tofu and edamame. Look for shelled bags of edamame alongside whole beans in the freezer section. To press tofu, cut the brick of tofu into three or four pieces, wrap the pieces in paper towels, and place a heavy object, such as a pot, on top of the pieces for about 10 minutes to remove as much water as possible. This will keep the tofu firm while cooking.

2 tablespoons sesame oil

2 cups frozen shelled edamame

1 cup sliced shiitake mushrooms

2 cups Everyday Vegetable Broth (page 92) or store-bought low-sodium broth

2 tablespoons cornstarch

2 tablespoons low-sodium soy sauce

1 (15-ounce) package extra-firm tofu, drained, pressed, and cut into ½-inch cubes

3 cups cooked brown rice, for serving

4 scallions, green and white parts, sliced, for serving

1. In a large skillet, heat the oil over medium heat. Add the edamame and mushrooms and cook for 5 to 7 minutes, stirring, until the mushrooms are browned and softened.

2. Meanwhile, in a small bowl, whisk together the broth, cornstarch, and soy sauce. Set aside.

3. Add the tofu to the skillet and cook for 3 to 5 minutes, until browned. Pour the broth mixture into the skillet and bring to a simmer for about 3 minutes, until the sauce is thickened. Serve over the rice topped with the scallions.

Tip: For a different flavor, substitute frozen lima beans for the edamame and cook as directed. To make this gluten-free, substitute tamari or coconut aminos for the soy sauce.

*Per Serving:* Calories: 340; Total fat: 11g; Protein: 19g; Carbohydrates: 41g; Fiber: 6g

# Mung Bean Dal

SERVES 6 / PREP TIME: 15 MINUTES / COOK TIME: 40 MINUTES

FREEZABLE / GLUTEN-FREE / NUT-FREE / SOY-FREE

Dal is an Indian dish prepared with lentils or other pulses and spices and is typically served with rice or flatbread like chapati, roti, or naan. This version uses mung beans, which, like lentils, are quick cooking and require no presoaking, making them perfect for this dish.

1 cup dried mung beans

4 cups water

1 tablespoon minced peeled fresh ginger

1 teaspoon ground turmeric

½ teaspoon salt

1 tablespoon avocado oil

2 teaspoons cumin seeds

1 onion, chopped

2 garlic cloves, minced

Juice from ½ lemon

2 tablespoons chopped fresh cilantro

1. In a large pot over high heat, cover the mung beans with the water. Add the ginger, turmeric, and salt. Bring to a boil; then reduce the heat to medium-low. Simmer for about 30 minutes, until the mung beans soften.

2. Meanwhile, heat the oil over medium-high heat. Stir in the cumin and cook for about 30 seconds, until fragrant. Add the onion and cook for about 5 minutes, until softened. Add the garlic and cook for about 30 seconds, until fragrant.

3. When the beans are done cooking, pour the onion mixture into the beans and mix well. Simmer for about 3 minutes, stirring. Add the lemon juice and cilantro and serve.

**Tip:** The term *dal* refers to both the split pulses (lentils, beans, and peas) and the soup-like dish made from them.

*Per Serving:* Calories: 155; Total fat: 3g; Protein: 9g; Carbohydrates: 25g; Fiber: 6g

# Sesame Chickpeas and Rice

Sesame chicken is a takeout favorite, and this alternative version featuring chickpeas does not disappoint. Maple syrup lightly sweetens the sauce to coat the chickpeas. This recipe doubles nicely and can be stored for up to 5 days, so make extra and enjoy easy lunches all week long.

½ cup Everyday Vegetable Broth (page 92) or store-bought low-sodium broth

1 tablespoon cornstarch

1 tablespoon extra-virgin olive oil

3 garlic cloves, minced

3 tablespoons low-sodium soy sauce

3 tablespoons pure maple syrup

1 tablespoon sesame oil

2 teaspoons rice vinegar

1 tablespoon grated peeled fresh ginger

3 cups cooked chickpeas or 2 (15-ounce) cans, drained and rinsed

2 scallions, green and white parts, sliced

2 tablespoons sesame seeds

2½ cups cooked brown rice

1. In a small bowl, stir together the broth and cornstarch and set aside.

2. In a large skillet, heat the oil over medium heat. Add the garlic and sauté for 30 seconds, until fragrant. Add the soy sauce, maple syrup, sesame oil, rice vinegar, and ginger and mix well. Bring to a simmer; then add in the broth mixture and simmer for 2 to 3 minutes, until thickened.

3. Add the chickpeas and cook for 2 to 3 minutes, until heated through. Sprinkle with the scallions and sesame seeds and serve with the rice.

**Tip:** While this dish is not typically spicy, it does taste great with a little added heat as well. Add red pepper flakes, if desired.

*Per Serving:* Calories: 343; Total fat: 10g; Protein: 11g; Carbohydrates: 55g; Fiber: 8g

# Roasted Kabocha Squash with Chickpeas

SERVES 4 / PREP TIME: 10 MINUTES / COOK TIME: 40 MINUTES

5 INGREDIENT / GLUTEN-FREE / NUT-FREE / SOY-FREE

I love winter squash—acorn, butternut, and pumpkin—and I really love kabocha squash. It's a squat Japanese squash that cooks up more quickly than some other squashes, and the skin is edible. Serve the roasted squash wedges and chickpeas over a bed of greens for a salad, or roll the filling up in a whole-grain wrap.

1 (2- to 3-pound) kabocha squash, washed well

2 tablespoons extra-virgin olive oil or aquafaba, divided

½ teaspoon salt

¼ teaspoon freshly ground black pepper

1½ cups cooked chickpeas or 1 (15-ounce) can, drained and rinsed

2 teaspoons smoked paprika

2 teaspoons garlic powder

1. Preheat the oven to 400°F. Line a baking sheet with parchment paper.
2. Halve the squash. Remove the seeds with a spoon and discard them. Remove the stem and then slice each half lengthwise to create 1-inch-thick wedges. Place the wedges on the prepared baking sheet. Drizzle 1 tablespoon of the oil over the squash. Toss with tongs to coat all sides. Sprinkle with the salt and pepper. Bake for 20 minutes.
3. While the squash bakes, in a medium bowl, combine the chickpeas with the remaining 1 tablespoon oil, paprika, and garlic powder. Toss gently, coating well.
4. Remove the baking sheet from the oven. Flip the squash over and pour the chickpeas onto the baking sheet, spreading them into a single layer around the squash. Bake for 15 to 20 minutes more, until the chickpeas are just beginning to brown and the squash is tender. Serve.

**Tip:** For an oil-free option, replace the oil with an equal amount of aquafaba (bean liquid).

**Tip:** For omnivores, consider adding a pound of seasoned boneless skinless chicken thighs to the baking sheet in step 4 and cook for 20 minutes, until the juices run clear.

*Per Serving:* Calories: 287; Total fat: 3g; Protein: 18g; Carbohydrates: 51g; Fiber: 17g

# Sweet Potato, Kale, and Black Bean Skillet

SERVES 4 / PREP TIME: 10 MINUTES / COOK TIME: 20 MINUTES

GLUTEN-FREE / NUT-FREE / QUICK / SOY-FREE

This skillet combines the complementary flavors of sweet potato, kale, and black beans to create a simple one-dish meal. Serve on its own or over crusty bread, rice, or quinoa or pair with a salad to finish out the meal.

2 tablespoons extra-virgin olive oil

1 large sweet potato, peeled and chopped

1½ cups cooked black beans or 1 (15-ounce) can, drained and rinsed

2 cups chopped stemmed kale

½ teaspoon ground cumin

½ teaspoon salt

¼ teaspoon freshly ground black pepper

Juice and grated zest of 1 lime

¼ cup chopped fresh cilantro

1. In a large skillet, heat the oil over medium-high heat. Add the sweet potato and sauté for 3 to 5 minutes, until it begins to brown. Cover, reduce the heat to medium-low, and cook for 6 to 8 minutes, until softened.

2. Add the beans and mix well. Stir in the kale, cumin, salt, and pepper. Cover and cook for 1 to 2 minutes; then stir again, until the kale is wilted and tender. Squeeze the lime juice over the top of the skillet and sprinkle with the lime zest and cilantro. Serve.

**Tip:** Give this a different smoky flavor by adding 1 teaspoon smoked paprika along with the cumin.

*Per Serving:* Calories: 196; Total fat: 7g; Protein: 7g; Carbohydrates: 27g; Fiber: 8g

# Scalloped Hearts of Palm and Adzuki Beans

SERVES 2 / PREP TIME: 10 MINUTES / COOK TIME: 25 MINUTES

GLUTEN-FREE / NUT-FREE / OIL-FREE / SOY-FREE

One of the fun things about cooking plant-based is getting creative. Hearts of palm and artichoke hearts are two vegetables that stand in beautifully for seafood. And if you cut hearts of palm into thick slices, they are a perfect replacement for scallops and contribute umami-rich flavor from the brine and a similar tender texture. Pinto and kidney beans can also be used in this recipe.

1 (14-ounce) can hearts of palm, drained

¼ cup balsamic vinegar

2 tablespoons minced shallot

3 garlic cloves, minced

1 large tomato, chopped

1½ cups cooked adzuki beans or 1 (15-ounce) can, drained and rinsed

½ cup red wine or red wine vinegar

Fresh parsley, for garnish (optional)

1. Cut the hearts of palm into ½-inch-thick rounds. Place them on a tea towel or paper towel and pat dry.
2. In a large nonstick skillet over high heat, sear the hearts of palm for 2 to 4 minutes on each side, until browned. Set aside.
3. In the same skillet over medium-high heat, combine the vinegar, shallot, and garlic and sauté for about 3 minutes, until tender. Add the tomato, beans, and wine and cook for about 8 minutes, stirring occasionally, until the mixture begins to gently bubble.
4. Reduce the heat to low. Gently nestle the hearts of palm into the mixture, cover, and simmer for 5 minutes. Remove from the heat. Garnish with parsley (if using) and serve.

*Per Serving:* Calories: 464; Total fat: 2g; Protein: 18g; Carbohydrates: 91g; Fiber: 4g

# Curried Chickpeas with Kale

This is a quick curried chickpea recipe that I usually make with canned chickpeas because it is so easy. It's a nice warming dish that is a favorite in my house all winter long. Serve it with quinoa or rice or on its own.

1 tablespoon extra-virgin olive oil

½ onion, diced

1 large carrot, diced

2 tablespoons curry powder

1½ teaspoons minced garlic

1 teaspoon grated peeled fresh ginger

½ teaspoon sweet paprika

½ teaspoon smoked paprika

¼ to ½ teaspoon ground cayenne pepper

4 cups chopped kale

3 cups cooked chickpeas or 2 (15-ounce) cans, drained and rinsed

1 (13.5-ounce) can full-fat coconut milk

½ cup Everyday Vegetable Broth (page 92) or store-bought low-sodium broth

½ teaspoon salt

Juice of 1 lime

1. In a large pot, heat the oil over medium-high heat. Add the onion and carrot and cook for about 5 minutes, until the onion is translucent. Add the curry powder, garlic, ginger, sweet paprika, smoked paprika, and cayenne. Cook, stirring constantly, for 30 seconds until the carrot and onion are coated and the spices are fragrant.

2. Add the kale, chickpeas, coconut milk, and broth. Bring to a boil; then reduce the heat to medium. Simmer for 15 minutes. Season with the salt, add the lime juice, and serve.

*Per Serving:* Calories: 277; Total fat: 16g; Protein: 8g; Carbohydrates: 28g; Fiber: 9g

# Smoky Black Beans with Turmeric Rice

SERVES 4 / PREP TIME: 10 MINUTES / COOK TIME: 50 MINUTES

GLUTEN-FREE / NUT-FREE / SOY-FREE

Rice and beans are classic vegetarian fare, and this fun twist is always a welcome addition at our table. Serve it with a green salad for a complete meal.

**2 tablespoons extra-virgin olive oil, divided**

**2 onions, diced, divided**

**1¾ cups Everyday Vegetable Broth (page 92) or store-bought low-sodium broth**

**1 cup brown rice, rinsed**

**1 teaspoon ground turmeric**

**1 teaspoon ground cumin**

**Salt**

**Freshly ground black pepper**

**1½ cups cooked black beans or 1 (15-ounce) can, drained and rinsed**

**1 tablespoon garlic powder**

**1½ teaspoons smoked paprika**

1. In a large saucepan, warm 1 tablespoon of oil over medium-high heat. Add half of the onions and sauté for 5 minutes, until softened. Add the broth, rice, turmeric, and cumin and bring to a boil. Season with salt and pepper.

2. Lower the heat to medium-low. Cover and cook for 40 minutes. Remove the pan from the heat and let it sit, covered, for 10 minutes.

3. Meanwhile, in another saucepan, warm the remaining 1 tablespoon of oil over medium-high heat. Add the remaining onions and sauté for about 5 minutes, until softened. Add the beans, garlic powder, and paprika and cook for about 5 minutes, until heated through. Season the bean mixture with salt and pepper. To serve, spoon the rice onto plates and top it with the beans.

**Tip:** Serve topped with sour cream or shredded cheese for a vegetarian option or with shredded chicken, pork, or beef for omnivores.

*Per Serving:* Calories: 357; Total fat: 64g; Protein: 11g; Carbohydrates: 64g; Fiber: 12g

# Black-Eyed Peas and Spinach Curry

SERVES 6 / PREP TIME: 10 MINUTES / COOK TIME: 20 MINUTES

GLUTEN-FREE / QUICK / SOY-FREE

There are many complicated recipes for making curries, but this simple blend is always a favorite of mine. Using just onion, garlic, ginger, curry powder, and coconut milk, this quick dish is perfect for a weeknight meal. If you can't find canned black-eyed peas, look for them in the freezer section of the grocery store.

2 tablespoons avocado oil

1 large onion, chopped

3 garlic cloves, minced

1 (1-inch) piece fresh ginger, peeled and grated or minced

3 cups cooked black-eyed peas or 2 (15-ounce) cans

1 tablespoon curry powder

1 teaspoon ground cayenne pepper (optional)

1 (15-ounce) can full-fat coconut milk

4 cups chopped fresh or frozen spinach

½ teaspoon salt

Freshly ground black pepper

3 cups cooked brown rice, for serving

1. In a large skillet, heat the oil over medium-high heat. Add the onion and cook for about 5 minutes, until softened. Add the garlic and ginger and cook, stirring, for about 30 seconds, until fragrant.

2. Stir in the black-eyed peas, curry powder, and cayenne (if using) and mix well. Add the coconut milk and bring to a simmer. Add the spinach and cook for about 5 minutes, until wilted. Season with the salt and pepper to taste. Serve over the rice.

**Tip:** This curry can be a great vehicle for any bits of leftover vegetables you have. Carrots, zucchini, kale, and peas can all be added to increase the vegetable content.

*Per Serving:* Calories: 395; Total fat: 19g; Protein: 11g; Carbohydrates: 49g; Fiber: 7g

# Buffalo Chickpea Quesadillas

SERVES 4 / PREP TIME: 10 MINUTES / COOK TIME: 20 MINUTES

QUICK / SOY-FREE

The creamy Buffalo sauce in this quesadilla is made using homemade cashew sauce and hot sauce to create the cheesy Buffalo flavor without the dairy. These are an easy weeknight meal or perfect when packed for lunch the next day. To save on prep time, replace the homemade cashew sauce with a store-bought alternative. (My favorite is Core and Rind Cashew Cheesy Sauce, which doesn't have added salt, oil, or sugar.)

1 tablespoon extra-virgin olive oil

1 onion, chopped

1 cup Creamy Cashew Sauce (page 94)

¼ cup chunky salsa

¼ cup Frank's RedHot sauce

1½ cups cooked chickpeas or 1 (15-ounce) can, drained and rinsed

1 bunch scallions, green part only, sliced

Olive oil cooking spray

4 (10-inch) whole-grain tortillas

1. In a large skillet, heat the oil over medium-high heat. Add the onion and cook for about 5 minutes, until softened.

2. In a small bowl, combine the cashew sauce, salsa, and hot sauce and mix well. Set aside.

3. Add the chickpeas to the skillet and mix with the onion. Pour the cashew sauce mixture into the skillet and stir for 1 to 2 minutes, until bubbly and thickened. Remove from the heat and stir in the scallions.

4. Heat another skillet over medium-high heat and spray with cooking spray. Place a tortilla in the pan and place half of the chickpea mixture over the tortilla in an even layer and nearly out to the edges. Top with another tortilla. Cook for 1 to 2 minutes, until toasted; then flip and cook for 1 to 2 minutes on the other side, until toasted. Repeat with the remaining chickpea mixture and tortillas.

5. Cut into quarters and serve.

Tip: Because RedHot is a milder hot sauce, it is used generously here, but if you use a hotter sauce, such as one with habanero, add a teaspoon or two at a time to create a sauce with a heat level that works for you.

*Per Serving:* Calories: 560; Total fat: 28g; Protein: 18g; Carbohydrates: 65g; Fiber: 12g

# Sweet Potato and Black Bean Burgers

SERVES 4 / PREP TIME: 10 MINUTES / COOK TIME: 25 MINUTES

FREEZABLE / NUT-FREE / SOY-FREE

These veggie burgers have a firm texture on account of the brown rice and sunflower seeds that bulk them up. The sweet potato is quickly cooked in the microwave in this recipe, but if you have leftover roasted sweet potatoes, you can substitute them here and save even more time. Serve topped with your favorite burger fixings like vegan mayo, mustard, lettuce, and tomato.

1 large sweet potato, unpeeled

1½ cups cooked black beans or 1 (15-ounce) can, drained and rinsed

1¼ cups cooked brown rice

½ cup coarsely chopped sunflower seeds

¼ cup minced red onion

2 teaspoons ground cumin

Salt

Freshly ground black pepper

2 tablespoons extra-virgin olive oil

4 whole-grain hamburger buns

1. Cover the sweet potato with a damp paper towel to keep moist during cooking. In a microwave, cook the sweet potato for 6 to 10 minutes, depending on the size of the sweet potato and your microwave, until it can be easily pierced with a fork. Remove and set aside to cool.

2. In a medium bowl, combine the beans, rice, sunflower seeds, onion, and cumin. Mash some of the beans with a spoon or potato masher.

3. When cool enough to handle, peel the sweet potato and mix it into the bowl until the ingredients are well combined. Season with salt and pepper.

4. Shape the mixture into four larger patties or eight smaller ones.

5. In a large skillet, heat the oil over medium heat. Add the burgers and cook for 4 to 6 minutes on each side, until browned. Serve on a bun.

**Tip:** Substitute white beans for the black beans in these burgers if desired. Because they are softer than black beans, only lightly mash the white beans to leave a bit of texture in the finished product, as they will fall apart even more when mixing.

*Per Serving:* Calories: 527; Total fat: 20g; Protein: 17g; Carbohydrates: 75g; Fiber: 14g

# "Crab Cake" Burgers

SERVES 6 / PREP TIME: 15 MINUTES / COOK TIME: 10 MINUTES

NUT-FREE

Switch up burger night with these delicious "crab cakes" made from chickpeas and hearts of palm, which add a seafood-like flavor to this dish that is reminiscent of real crab. You can use just chickpeas if that's all you have, but I like the addition of hearts of palm, which mimic the shredded texture of crab.

1½ cups cooked chickpeas or 1 (15-ounce) can, drained and rinsed

1 (14-ounce) can hearts of palm, drained and coarsely chopped

1 celery stalk, finely diced

2 scallions, green and white parts, chopped

2 tablespoons Old Bay seasoning

1 tablespoon low-sodium soy sauce

1 teaspoon freshly squeezed lemon juice

¾ cup bread crumbs

3 tablespoons extra-virgin olive oil

6 whole-grain hamburger buns

12 large iceberg lettuce leaves

¼ cup vegan mayonnaise (optional)

1. In a large bowl, combine the chickpeas and hearts of palm. Using a fork or a potato masher, mash both into small chunks. Alternatively, you could do this in a food processor.

2. Add the celery, scallions, Old Bay, soy sauce, and lemon juice and mix well. Stir in the bread crumbs. Divide the mixture into six even portions and, using your hands, form them into patties about ¾ inch thick.

3. In a large sauté pan or skillet, heat the oil over medium-high heat until shimmering. Add the patties and panfry for 3 minutes per side, or until crispy on the outside. Serve on burger buns topped with the lettuce and mayonnaise (if using).

*Per Serving:* Calories: 325; Total fat: 11g; Protein: 13g; Carbohydrates: 46g; Fiber: 8g

# Quinoa Tabbouleh with White Bean Patties

SERVES 4 / PREP TIME: 15 MINUTES / COOK TIME: 30 MINUTES

NUT-FREE / SOY-FREE

Tabbouleh is Levantine salad, traditionally made with bulgur and finely chopped fresh herbs. In this version, nutrient-dense quinoa is used to make the salad and crispy white bean patties top it to make a protein-packed main course.

1 cup quinoa

2 cups water

¼ cup freshly squeezed lemon juice

4 tablespoons extra-virgin olive oil, divided

Salt

6 scallions, green and white parts, sliced, divided

½ cup chopped fresh parsley

¼ cup chopped fresh mint

1 seedless cucumber, chopped

1 cup cherry tomatoes, chopped

Freshly ground black pepper

1½ cups cooked white beans (cannellini, navy, or great northern) or 1 (15-ounce) can, drained and rinsed

½ cup panko bread crumbs

1. Place the quinoa in a fine-mesh sieve and rinse under cold water for 2 to 3 minutes, or until the cloudy water becomes clear.

2. In a small pot over high heat, combine the water and quinoa and bring to a boil; then reduce the heat to low. Cover and simmer for about 15 minutes, until the water is absorbed and the quinoa is tender.

3. Transfer the quinoa to a large bowl and toss with the lemon juice, 3 tablespoons of oil, and 1 teaspoon of salt. Fold in half of the scallions, the parsley, mint, cucumber, and tomatoes. Season with additional salt and pepper. Transfer to the refrigerator to cool while you make the patties.

4. In a large bowl, combine the beans, the remaining half of the scallions, and the bread crumbs. Using a potato masher, smash the beans until just a few chunks remain. Season lightly with salt and pepper.

5. Form the mixture into eight small patties. In a large skillet, heat the remaining 1 tablespoon of oil over medium-high heat. Add the patties and cook for 2 to 3 minutes per side, until crisp and browned. Serve the tabbouleh topped with the bean patties.

---

**Tip:** If you want to add a little heat to the bean patties, add 1 or 2 teaspoons harissa paste to the mixture before frying.

*Per Serving:* Calories: 436; Total fat: 17g; Protein: 15g; Carbohydrates: 61g; Fiber: 13g

# Southwestern Black Bean Pasta

SERVES 4 / PREP TIME: 10 MINUTES / COOK TIME: 15 MINUTES

NUT-FREE / QUICK / SOY-FREE

This dish packs a punch of flavor. Seeding the jalapeño pepper keeps the heat to a minimum, but you can substitute a poblano pepper to make this milder.

8 ounces whole-grain penne pasta

Olive oil cooking spray

1 onion, chopped

1 jalapeño pepper, seeded and chopped

1 teaspoon minced garlic

1½ teaspoons cornstarch

1 teaspoon chili powder

1 teaspoon smoked paprika

Salt

Freshly ground black pepper

¾ cup Everyday Vegetable Broth (page 92) or store-bought low-sodium broth

1½ cups cooked black beans or 1 (15-ounce) can, drained and rinsed

2 cups frozen corn, thawed

2 cups quartered cherry tomatoes

1. Bring a large pot of salted water to a boil over high heat. Add the pasta and cook according to the package directions until tender, usually about 10 minutes. Scoop out and reserve ⅓ cup of the cooking water; then drain the pasta.

2. Meanwhile, coat a large skillet with cooking spray and set it over medium heat. Add the onion and jalapeño and sauté for 7 minutes. Add the garlic and sauté for 1 minute more. Sprinkle in the cornstarch, chili powder, and paprika and stir. Season the mixture with salt and pepper.

3. Add the broth, beans, corn, and tomatoes and bring the mixture to a boil. Lower the heat to medium-low and simmer until thickened, about 3 minutes. Add the pasta and the reserved cooking water, 1 tablespoon at a time, until the pasta is the desired consistency. Serve warm.

*Per Serving:* Calories: 425; Total fat: 2g; Protein: 17g; Carbohydrates: 87g; Fiber: 14g

# Fava Bean and Arugula Linguine

SERVES 6 / PREP TIME: 10 MINUTES / COOK TIME: 15 MINUTES

5 INGREDIENT / QUICK / SOY-FREE

Fava beans are deliciously addictive when they are young, fresh, and buttery. This pasta recipe pairs them with peppery arugula and lemon juice to create a bright dish that shines. Toasted pine nuts add an additional layer of flavor.

**16 ounces whole-grain linguine pasta**

**¼ cup pine nuts**

**1½ cups shelled fresh or thawed frozen fava beans**

**2 tablespoons extra-virgin olive oil**

**3 cups arugula**

**Juice and grated zest of 1 lemon**

**½ teaspoon salt**

**¼ teaspoon freshly ground black pepper**

1. Bring a large pot of salted water to a boil over medium heat. Cook the pasta according to package directions until tender, usually about 7 minutes. Using a strainer, remove the pasta from the water, leaving the water to boil on the stove.

2. While the pasta is cooking, in a small, dry skillet, toast the pine nuts over medium-low for about 5 minutes, until lightly browned. Remove from the pan and set aside.

3. Add the fava beans to the boiling water and cook for about 2 minutes, until bright green. Drain the water.

4. In a large bowl, toss the pasta, fava beans, and pine nuts. Stir in the oil, arugula, lemon juice, and lemon zest. Season with the salt and pepper and serve.

**Tip:** Fava beans can be replaced with fresh or frozen green peas if you can't find favas.

*Per Serving:* Calories: 373; Total fat: 11g; Protein: 14g; Carbohydrates: 62g; Fiber: 9g

# Black Bean and Corn Bread Casserole

SERVES 6 / PREP TIME: 15 MINUTES / COOK TIME: 40 MINUTES

NUT-FREE / SOY-FREE

This simple dish combines corn bread and black beans in one pan for an easy and delicious weeknight meal. Black beans are seasoned with onion, garlic, cilantro, and cumin and topped with a layer of corn bread for a simple yet filling meal. Serve with a green salad.

**FOR THE BLACK BEANS**

1 tablespoon extra-virgin olive oil

1 large onion, chopped

1 red bell pepper, chopped

1 celery stalk, finely chopped

3 garlic cloves, minced

1½ cups cooked black beans or 1 (15-ounce) can, drained and rinsed

1 large tomato, chopped

¼ cup chopped fresh cilantro

½ teaspoon ground cumin

Olive oil cooking spray

**FOR THE CORN BREAD TOPPING**

1 cup yellow cornmeal

1 cup whole wheat flour

1 teaspoon baking powder

¼ teaspoon salt

1 cup unsweetened plant-based milk

¼ cup avocado oil

3 tablespoons pure maple syrup

1. Preheat the oven to 350°F.

2. **MAKE THE BLACK BEANS:** In a large skillet, heat the olive oil over medium-high heat. Add the onion, bell pepper, and celery and sauté for about 5 minutes, until softened. Add the garlic and cook for about 30 seconds, until fragrant. Add the beans, tomato, cilantro, and cumin and mix well.

3. Spray a 9-inch baking dish with cooking spray. Transfer the beans to the prepared dish and spread in an even layer. Set aside.

4. **MAKE THE CORN BREAD TOPPING:** In a large bowl, mix the cornmeal, flour, baking powder, and salt. Stir in the milk, oil, and maple syrup and mix until combined.

5. Spread the corn bread mixture over the beans in an even layer. Cook for 25 to 30 minutes, until golden brown. Cut into six pieces and serve.

**Tip:** If you eat dairy, this is great topped with shredded cheese or a dollop of sour cream. If not, the Plant-Based Sour Cream (page 93) works well spooned over the top.

*Per Serving:* Calories: 355; Total fat: 13g; Protein: 9g; Carbohydrates: 53g; Fiber: 9g

# Pinto Bean and Cremini Mushroom Burritos with Cilantro Sour Cream

SERVES 6 / PREP TIME: 15 MINUTES / COOK TIME: 25 MINUTES

NUT-FREE

These burritos are smothered and baked for a crisp exterior that is *so* good. These are great straight out of the oven, but they also reheat well, making them perfect for leftovers.

1 tablespoon extra-virgin olive oil

1 onion, chopped

1 cup sliced cremini mushrooms

3 garlic cloves, minced

2 teaspoons sweet paprika

1 teaspoon ground cumin

1 tablespoon tomato paste

1½ cups cooked pinto beans or 1 (15-ounce) can, drained and rinsed

1 cup cooked brown rice

½ teaspoon salt

¼ teaspoon freshly ground black pepper

6 (10-inch) whole-grain flour tortillas

¼ cup Plant-Based Sour Cream (page 93) or store-bought

1 tablespoon chopped fresh cilantro

Salsa, for serving

1. Preheat the oven to 350°F.
2. In a large skillet, heat the oil over medium-high heat. Add the onion and mushrooms and cook for about 5 minutes, until softened. Add the garlic, paprika, and cumin and cook for about 30 seconds, until fragrant. Stir in the tomato paste and mix to combine. Stir in the beans and rice and season with the salt and pepper.
3. Working on a clean surface, spoon the mixture into each tortilla; then fold in the sides of the tortilla and roll up to close. Place them seam-side down on a baking sheet. Repeat with the remaining tortillas and filling.
4. In a small bowl, mix the sour cream and cilantro. Spread this over the top of the burritos and bake for about 15 minutes, until golden brown and crisp. Serve topped with salsa.

**Tip:** If you like heat, add up to 1 teaspoon of chipotle powder to the filling.

*Per Serving:* Calories: 357; Total fat: 10g; Protein: 12g; Carbohydrates: 59g; Fiber: 10g

# White Bean, Mushroom, and Kale Potpie

SERVES 6 / PREP TIME: 15 MINUTES / COOK TIME: 50 MINUTES
SOY-FREE

The flaky crust is my favorite part about a potpie. Paired with this simple, vegetable-packed filling of carrot, kale, mushrooms, and creamy white beans, this is a nourishing meal. The homemade crust is easy to make, but you can use store-bought to save a bit of time if you like.

**FOR THE CRUST**

1⅓ cups whole wheat flour

½ teaspoon salt

½ cup refined coconut oil, at room temperature

6 to 7 tablespoons ice water

**FOR THE FILLING**

2 tablespoons extra-virgin olive oil

1 large onion, chopped

3 garlic cloves, minced

3 cups cooked white beans (cannellini, navy, or great northern) or 2 (15-ounce) cans, drained and rinsed

1 cup sliced cremini mushrooms

1 carrot, finely chopped

½ teaspoon dried thyme

1 tablespoon whole wheat flour

6 cups chopped or baby kale

1 cup Everyday Vegetable Broth (page 92) or store-bought low-sodium broth

1. Preheat the oven to 350°F.

2. **MAKE THE CRUST:** In a large bowl, mix together the flour and salt. Using two forks, cut in the coconut oil and combine until the mixture is in small pieces.

3. Stir in the ice water, 1 tablespoon at a time, until the dough comes together and is smooth but not sticky. Form it into a ball, cover with plastic wrap, and press into a disc. Refrigerate until the filling is ready.

4. **MAKE THE FILLING:** In a large skillet, heat the oil over medium-high heat. Add the onion and sauté for about 5 minutes, until softened. Add the garlic and cook for about 30 seconds, until fragrant.

5. Stir in the beans, mushrooms, carrot, and thyme. Cook, stirring once or twice, for about 5 minutes, until the carrots are barely softened and the vegetables are lightly browned.

6. Reduce the heat to low and stir in the flour. Mix well to coat the vegetables. Stir in the kale and broth and bring to a simmer. Cover and cook for 2 to 3 minutes, until the kale is wilted. Remove the top and let the vegetables simmer for 1 to 2 minutes, until the sauce is thickened. Pour the filling into a 9-inch baking dish or pie pan.

7. On a floured surface, roll out the dough large enough to cover the dish. Drape the crust over the dish, crimping the edges to form a seal. Cut two or three slits in the top of the pie. Bake for 25 to 30 minutes, until browned and crispy. Let cool for about 10 minutes before serving.

---

**Tip:** If you don't have refined coconut oil, use another neutral vegetable oil instead. Unrefined coconut oil will work, too, but will have a strong coconut flavor.

*Per Serving:* Calories: 468; Total fat: 25g; Protein: 13g; Carbohydrates: 50g; Fiber: 15g

# Lentil Shepherd's Pie

SERVES 4 / PREP TIME: 5 MINUTES / COOK TIME: 35 MINUTES

GLUTEN-FREE / NUT-FREE / SOY-FREE

This lentil version of shepherd's pie is an easy, satisfying meal that requires very little actual hands-on time. Notice that I'm asking you to leave the peel on the potatoes. Of course, you can do whatever you want, but for this recipe, I like how the peel keeps the pie pieces together. Besides, we're all too busy to peel veggies, aren't we?

Olive oil cooking spray

1 pound russet potatoes, unpeeled and cubed

1 teaspoon extra-virgin olive oil

12 ounces fresh or frozen green beans

1½ cups cooked lentils or 1 (15-ounce) can, drained and rinsed

2 tablespoons vegan Worcestershire sauce

¾ cup unsweetened plant-based milk, divided

½ teaspoon salt

¼ teaspoon freshly ground black pepper

1. Preheat the oven to 400°F. Spray an 8-inch square baking pan with 2-inch sides with cooking spray.

2. In a large saucepan or pot, cover the potatoes with water. Bring to a boil over high heat; then boil for 10 to 15 minutes, until they are tender.

3. Meanwhile, in a large skillet, heat the oil over medium-high heat. Add the green beans and cook for 1 minute. Add the lentils, Worcestershire sauce, and ½ cup of milk, and stir well. Bring to a boil; then cover and cook for 3 minutes longer. Transfer to the baking pan.

4. Drain the potatoes and return to the pot. Add the remaining ¼ cup of milk and the salt and mash with a potato masher. Spread the mashed potatoes over the lentil mixture. Sprinkle with the pepper. Bake until the lentils are bubbling, about 15 minutes. Serve with additional salt and pepper.

**Tip:** Feel free to add other veggies, like chopped celery, onions, carrots, asparagus, spinach, or corn, to the skillet with the green beans in step 3.

*Per Serving:* Calories: 336; Total fat: 3g; Protein: 19g; Carbohydrates: 61g; Fiber: 13g

CHAPTER SIX

# STAPLES AND SWEETS

< Chocolate Hummus, page 97

# Everyday Vegetable Broth

MAKES ABOUT 8 CUPS / PREP TIME: 5 MINUTES / COOK TIME: 45 MINUTES

FREEZABLE / GLUTEN-FREE / NUT-FREE / OIL-FREE / SOY-FREE

You likely have many of these ingredients around most of the time, and that means that any day of the week, you could easily pull together a simple, flavorful broth. I use it for soups and stews as well as to spoon into dishes for a little extra liquid during cooking. And, of course, this is perfect for any recipe in this book calling for vegetable broth.

8 cups water

4 large carrots, coarsely chopped

4 celery stalks, coarsely chopped

1 cup sliced cremini mushrooms

1 apple of choice, quartered (include the peel and core)

4 to 6 garlic cloves, unpeeled and halved

1 teaspoon black peppercorns

2 sprigs thyme or 1 teaspoon dried thyme

2 bay leaves

1. In a large pot, combine the water, carrots, celery, mushrooms, apple, garlic, peppercorns, thyme, and bay leaves. Bring to a low boil over high heat. Once boiling, reduce the heat to low and simmer for 40 minutes.

2. Strain the broth through a fine-mesh strainer or cheesecloth and discard the solids. This can be prepared up to 1 week in advance and refrigerated in an airtight container or frozen in a zip-top freezer bag for 3 to 6 months.

**Tip:** Pull out your trusty pressure cooker! Add all the ingredients to a steamer basket and set it in the pot. Cover with the water. Lock the lid and cook on high pressure for 15 minutes. Use a natural release. Pull the basket out and you've strained the broth.

*Per Serving (1 cup):* Calories: 40; Total fat: 0g; Protein: 2g; Carbohydrates: 8g; Fiber: 2g

# Plant-Based Sour Cream

MAKES 1 CUP / PREP TIME: 5 MINUTES

5 INGREDIENT / GLUTEN-FREE / NO COOK / NUT-FREE / OIL-FREE / QUICK

Dairy-based sour cream is easily replaced with this plant-based variety loaded with great flavor without the dairy. Using silken tofu to mimic the texture of the original, this version is also high in protein. Adding a dollop of this plant-powered sour cream to your tacos or burrito bowls will truly do the body good.

**8 ounces silken tofu**

**2 tablespoons freshly squeezed lemon juice**

**1 teaspoon apple cider vinegar**

**1 teaspoon onion powder**

**¼ teaspoon salt**

In a blender, combine the tofu, lemon juice, vinegar, onion powder, and salt. Blend for 1 minute, or until the mixture reaches a creamy consistency. Store in an airtight container in the refrigerator for 3 to 5 days.

*Per Serving (1 tablespoon):* Calories: 10; Total fat: 0g; Protein: 1g; Carbohydrates: 1g; Fiber: 0g

# Creamy Cashew Sauce

MAKES 1½ CUPS / PREP TIME: 5 MINUTES, PLUS 15 MINUTES TO SOAK / COOK TIME: 5 MINUTES

5 INGREDIENT / GLUTEN-FREE / OIL-FREE / QUICK / SOY-FREE

This sauce is easy to put together and can be customized with add-ins to give it different flavors, like in the Buffalo Chickpea Quesadillas (page 78). Use it in nachos or any other dish where you want to achieve a cheesy flavor.

**1½ cups raw unsalted cashews**

**1 small carrot, coarsely chopped**

**¼ cup sesame seeds**

**2 garlic cloves**

**1 teaspoon dried onion flakes**

**1 teaspoon salt**

**1 cup water, plus more as needed**

1. Place the cashews in a small pot and cover with water. Bring to a boil over high heat; then remove from the heat and let soak for 15 minutes. Drain the water and rinse well.

2. In a blender or food processor, combine the soaked cashews, carrot, sesame seeds, garlic, onion, and salt. Pour the water over the cashews and blend for about 1 minute, until smooth. Add more water as needed to create a pourable sauce. Store in an airtight container in the refrigerator for 3 to 5 days.

**Tip:** Stir a cup of salsa into a cup of this sauce for delicious plant-based queso salsa dip.

**Tip:** If you are planning ahead, instead of the quick soak method used here, you can cover the cashews in cool water and soak for 2 to 4 hours. Drain and proceed as directed.

*Per Serving (¼ cup):* Calories: 225; Total fat: 18g; Protein: 7g; Carbohydrates: 12g; Fiber: 2g

# Plant-Based Parmesan

MAKES ABOUT ½ CUP / PREP TIME: 5 MINUTES

5 INGREDIENT / GLUTEN-FREE / NO COOK / NUT-FREE / OIL-FREE / QUICK / SOY-FREE

This cheesy-crunchy topping is great sprinkled on pastas or soups. It's particularly nice on Creamy Cauliflower and White Bean Soup with Herbed Croutons (page 57) and the Fava Bean and Arugula Linguine (page 83). You can switch it up every time by using whatever nuts or seeds you like. In fact, if you use ground almonds or hemp seeds, you don't need a blender.

½ cup seeds or nuts, such as sunflower, pumpkin, sesame, or hemp seeds or walnuts, cashews, or almonds

½ cup nutritional yeast

Pinch salt

In a blender, pulse the seeds or nuts until crumbly. Add the nutritional yeast and salt, and pulse a few more times. Store in an airtight container at room temperature for up to 1 week.

**Tip:** For even more flavor, add ¼ teaspoon of both onion powder and garlic powder.

*Per Serving (2 tablespoons) Calories:* 203; Total fat: 15g; Protein: 11g; Carbohydrates: 11g; Fiber: 6g

# Vanilla Date Shake

SERVES 4 / PREP TIME: 5 MINUTES

5 INGREDIENT / GLUTEN-FREE / NO COOK / NUT-FREE / OIL-FREE / QUICK / SOY-FREE

Chickpeas are an amazing addition to this shake because they will keep you going for hours with their fiber-rich, protein-dense nutritional profile, yet their mild flavor disappears right into the vanilla creaminess. Use this yummy shake as a mini-meal anytime you need a boost.

1½ cups cooked chickpeas or 1 (15-ounce) can, drained and rinsed

10 pitted dates

1 tablespoon vanilla extract

2¼ cups unsweetened plant-based milk, plus more as needed

3 large frozen bananas

Pinch salt (optional)

In a blender, combine the chickpeas, dates, vanilla, milk, bananas, and salt (if using) and process until completely smooth. If you need more liquid, add a little more milk and process to combine. Enjoy immediately.

**Tip:** If you don't have a high-speed blender, soak the dates in the milk for several hours in the refrigerator so they soften enough to blend smooth.

**Tip:** If you want an even easier version of this shake, you can omit the dates and add a dash of sweetener, such as maple syrup, instead.

*Per Serving:* Calories: 278; Total fat: 4g; Protein: 7g; Carbohydrates: 56g; Fiber: 9g

# Chocolate Hummus

MAKES ABOUT 2 CUPS / PREP TIME: 10 MINUTES

5 INGREDIENT / GLUTEN-FREE / NO COOK / NUT-FREE / OIL-FREE / QUICK / SOY-FREE

Unlike most desserts, this luxurious chocolate hummus doesn't have added oils, refined sweeteners, or flours. Plus, it has the added iron, protein, and fiber of chickpeas as well as the antioxidants of cacao. This chocolate hummus is great plain, but it's also delicious as a dip for strawberries or bananas. Or you can serve it topped with some chocolate chips and a dollop of peanut butter for extra pizzazz.

**1½ cups cooked chickpeas or 1 (15-ounce) can, drained and rinsed**

**¼ cup cacao powder**

**6 tablespoons pure maple syrup**

**¼ cup unsweetened vanilla plant-based milk, plus more as needed**

**1 tablespoon vanilla extract**

**½ teaspoon salt**

1. In a blender or food processor, combine the chickpeas, cacao powder, maple syrup, milk, vanilla, and salt. Blend until as smooth as possible. You will likely have enough liquid to blend, but if not, add 1 or 2 tablespoons of milk. (I've found certain brands of chickpeas require more.)

2. Once velvety smooth, serve immediately, or store in an airtight container in the refrigerator for up to 1 week.

*Per Serving (⅓ cup):* Calories: 133; Total fat: 3g; Protein: 5g; Carbohydrates: 28g; Fiber: 4g

# Chocolate Chip Chickpea Blondies

MAKES 16 BLONDIES / PREP TIME: 15 MINUTES / COOK TIME: 30 MINUTES
GLUTEN-FREE / SOY-FREE

Beans are not just for the main course! They can also form the base of baked goods, like in these chickpea blondies. Formed in a pan like a brownie, blondies are the equivalent of a chocolate chip cookie bar, and this gluten-free version is delicious—and sweetened with natural sugars only.

Olive oil cooking spray

1½ cups cooked chickpeas or 1 (15-ounce) can, drained and rinsed

⅓ cup pure maple syrup

¼ cup natural peanut butter

¼ cup oat flour

1 teaspoon vanilla extract

1 teaspoon baking powder

¼ teaspoon salt

½ cup vegan refined-sugar-free dark chocolate chips, such as Lily's Sweets or Pascha brands

1. Preheat the oven to 350°F. Spray an 8-inch baking dish with cooking spray and set aside.
2. In a food processor, combine the chickpeas, maple syrup, peanut butter, oat flour, vanilla, baking powder, and salt. Process until smooth, scraping the sides as you go. Stir in the chocolate chips.
3. Transfer the batter to the prepared baking dish and spread evenly. Bake for about 30 minutes, until lightly browned. The blondies will firm up as they cool. Cut into 16 pieces and serve.

**Tip:** Add ½ cup of chopped pecans or walnuts to add a little crunch to the blondies.

**Tip:** It's incredibly easy to make your own oat flour. Simply process an equal amount of rolled oats in a blender or food processor until finely ground into a flour consistency.

*Per Serving (1 blondie):* Calories: 107; Total fat: 5g; Protein: 3g; Carbohydrates: 13g; Fiber: 2g

# Bean Cooking Quick Reference Guide

**Note:** All slow cooker times are for a low setting unless otherwise noted.

| BEAN/LEGUME (1 CUP) | SOAK TIME | COOK TIME | WATER (CUPS) | YIELD (CUPS) |
|---|---|---|---|---|
| Adzuki beans | 2–3 hours | **Stovetop:** 45–55 minutes<br>**Pressure cooker:** 20–25 minutes (unsoaked) or 5–9 minutes (soaked); 20 minutes natural release<br>**Slow cooker:** 4–6 hours on low or 3 hours on high | 4 | 3 |
| Black beans | 4–8 hours | **Stovetop:** 60–90 minutes<br>**Pressure cooker:** 20–30 minutes (unsoaked) or 4–8 minutes (soaked); 20 minutes natural release<br>**Slow cooker:** 6–8 hours | 4 | 2¼ |
| Black-eyed peas | 2–3 hours (optional) | **Stovetop:** 35–45 minutes<br>**Pressure cooker:** 15 minutes; 20 minutes natural release<br>**Slow cooker:** 6–8 hours | 3 | 2 |
| Cannellini beans | 4–8 hours | **Stovetop:** 1 hour<br>**Pressure cooker:** 30 minutes (unsoaked) or 8–10 minutes (soaked); 20 minutes natural release<br>**Slow cooker:** not recommended | 3 | 2½ |
| Chickpeas | 8–12 hours | **Stovetop:** 1–3 hours<br>**Pressure cooker:** 35–40 minutes (unsoaked) or 10–15 minutes (soaked); 20 minutes natural release<br>**Slow cooker:** 6–8 hours on low or 3–6 hours on high (unsoaked) | 4 | 2 |
| Cranberry beans | 4–8 hours | **Stovetop:** 90 minutes<br>**Pressure cooker:** 25–30 minutes; 20 minutes natural release<br>**Slow cooker:** 6–8 hours on low or 4–5 hours on high | 3 | 3 |
| Fava beans | 8–12 hours | **Stovetop:** 40–50 minutes<br>**Pressure cooker:** 8–10 minutes; 20 minutes natural release<br>**Slow cooker:** 8–10 hours on low or 4–5 hours on high | 3 | 1⅔ |

| BEAN/LEGUME (1 CUP) | SOAK TIME | COOK TIME | WATER (CUPS) | YIELD (CUPS) |
|---|---|---|---|---|
| Gigante beans | 8–12 hours | **Stovetop:** 1 hour<br>**Pressure cooker:** 50 minutes; 20 minutes natural release<br>**Slow cooker:** 8–10 hours on low or 4–6 hours on high | 4 | 3 |
| Great northern beans | 4–8 hours | **Stovetop:** 1½ hours<br>**Pressure cooker:** 25–30 minutes (unsoaked) or 8–10 minutes (soaked); 15 minutes natural release<br>**Slow cooker:** 7–8 hours on low or 3 hours on high | 3½ | 2⅔ |
| Kidney beans | 4–8 hour | **Stovetop:** 1 hour<br>**Pressure cooker:** 25–35 minutes (unsoaked) or 8–10 minutes (soaked); 20 minutes natural release<br>**Slow cooker:** not recommended | 3 | 2¼ |
| Lentils, brown | N/A | **Stovetop:** 15–20 minutes<br>**Pressure cooker:** 10–12 minutes; quick release<br>**Slow cooker:** 4 hours on low or 1½–2 hours on high | 2¼ | 2¼ |
| Lentils, green | N/A | **Stovetop:** 15–20 minutes<br>**Pressure cooker:** 10–12 minutes; quick release<br>**Slow cooker:** 4 hours on low or 1½ hours on high | 2 | 2 |
| Lentils, red | N/A | **Stovetop:** 15–20 minutes<br>**Pressure cooker:** 10 minutes; quick release<br>**Slow cooker:** 4 hours on low or 1½ hours on high | 3 | 2½ |
| Lima beans (butter beans), large | 8–12 hours | **Stovetop:** 45–60 minutes<br>**Pressure cooker:** 14 minutes; 20 minutes natural release<br>**Slow cooker:** 2 hours on high, then 4 hours on low | 4 | 2 |
| Lima beans (butter beans), small | 8–12 hours | **Stovetop:** 50–60 minutes<br>**Pressure cooker:** 7 minutes; 15 minutes natural release<br>**Slow cooker:** 2½ hours | 4 | 3 |

| BEAN/LEGUME (1 CUP) | SOAK TIME | COOK TIME | WATER (CUPS) | YIELD (CUPS) |
|---|---|---|---|---|
| Mung beans | N/A | **Stovetop:** 30 minutes<br>**Pressure cooker:** 20 minutes; 20 minutes natural release<br>**Slow cooker:** 6 hours on low or 3 hours on high | 2½ | 2 |
| Navy beans | 4–8 hours | **Stovetop:** 45–60 minutes<br>**Pressure cooker:** 20–25 minutes (unsoaked) or 8 minutes (soaked); 20 minutes natural release<br>**Slow cooker:** 5–6 hours on low or 3–4 hours on high | 3 | 2⅔ |
| Pinto beans | 4–8 hours | **Stovetop:** 60–90 minutes<br>**Pressure cooker:** 25–30 minutes (unsoaked) or 8–10 minutes (soaked); 20 minutes natural release<br>**Slow cooker:** 6–7 hours on low or 3 hours on high | 3 | 2⅔ |
| Soybeans | 8–12 hours | **Stovetop:** 1–3 hours<br>**Pressure cooker:** 35–45 minutes (unsoaked) or 20 minutes (soaked); 20 minutes natural release<br>**Slow cooker:** 6–8 hours on high | 4 | 3 |
| Split peas | N/A | **Stovetop:** 20–30 minutes<br>**Pressure cooker:** 15–20 minutes; 20 minutes natural release<br>**Slow cooker:** 4–5 hours on low or 2½ hours on high | 3 | 3 |

# Measurement Conversions

## VOLUME EQUIVALENTS (LIQUID)

| US STANDARD | US STANDARD (OUNCES) | METRIC (APPROXIMATE) |
| --- | --- | --- |
| 2 tablespoons | 1 fl. oz. | 30 mL |
| ¼ cup | 2 fl. oz. | 60 mL |
| ½ cup | 4 fl. oz. | 120 mL |
| 1 cup | 8 fl. oz. | 240 mL |
| 1½ cups | 12 fl. oz. | 355 mL |
| 2 cups or 1 pint | 16 fl. oz. | 475 mL |
| 4 cups or 1 quart | 32 fl. oz. | 1 L |
| 1 gallon | 128 fl. oz. | 4 L |

## VOLUME EQUIVALENTS (DRY)

| US STANDARD | METRIC (APPROXIMATE) |
| --- | --- |
| ⅛ teaspoon | 0.5 mL |
| ¼ teaspoon | 1 mL |
| ½ teaspoon | 2 mL |
| ¾ teaspoon | 4 mL |
| 1 teaspoon | 5 mL |
| 1 tablespoon | 15 mL |
| ¼ cup | 59 mL |
| ⅓ cup | 79 mL |
| ½ cup | 118 mL |
| ⅔ cup | 156 mL |
| ¾ cup | 177 mL |
| 1 cup | 235 mL |
| 2 cups or 1 pint | 475 mL |
| 3 cups | 700 mL |
| 4 cups or 1 quart | 1 L |

## OVEN TEMPERATURES

| FAHRENHEIT | CELSIUS (APPROXIMATE) |
| --- | --- |
| 250°F | 120°C |
| 300°F | 150°C |
| 325°F | 165°C |
| 350°F | 180°C |
| 375°F | 190°C |
| 400°F | 200°C |
| 425°F | 220°C |
| 450°F | 230°C |

## WEIGHT EQUIVALENTS

| US STANDARD | METRIC (APPROXIMATE) |
| --- | --- |
| ½ ounce | 15 g |
| 1 ounce | 30 g |
| 2 ounces | 60 g |
| 4 ounces | 115 g |
| 8 ounces | 225 g |
| 12 ounces | 340 g |
| 16 ounces or 1 pound | 455 g |

# References

Bazzano, L. A., J. He, L. G. Ogden, et al. "Legume Consumption and Risk of Coronary Heart Disease in US Men and Women: NHANES I Epidemiologic Follow-up Study." *Archives of Internal Medicine* 161, no. 21 (2001): 2573–78. doi.org/10.1001/archinte.161.21.2573.

The Bean Institute. "The Traditional Four-Step Method." Accessed December 16, 2020. BeanInstitute.com/the-traditional-four-step-method.

Chandler, Jenny. *The Better Bean Cookbook.* New York: Sterling Epicure, 2013.

Cleveland Clinic. "What You Should Know about Beans and the (Embarrassing) Gas They Cause." health.ClevelandClinic.org/the-musical-fruit-what-you-should-know-about-beans-and-gas.

Harvard Health Publishing. "Meat or Beans: What Will You Have? Part I: Meat." Accessed December 16, 2020. health.Harvard.edu/staying-healthy/meat-or-beans-what-will-you-have-part-i-meat.

Kristensen, Marlene D., et al. "Meals Based on Vegetable Protein Sources (Beans and Peas) Are More Satiating Than Meals Based on Animal Protein Sources (Veal and Pork): A Randomized Cross-Over Meal Test Study." *Food & Nutrition Research* 60 (October 2016): 19. doi.org/10.3402/fnr.v60.32634.

Kubala, Jillian. "Aquafaba: An Egg and Dairy Substitute Worth Trying?" Accessed December 15, 2020. Healthline.com/nutrition/aquafaba.

Mayo Clinic. "Weight Loss." Accessed December 15, 2020. MayoClinic.org/healthy-lifestyle/weight-loss/in-depth/weight-loss/art-20044318.

Messina, Virginia. "Nutritional and Health Benefits of Dried Beans." *American Journal of Clinical Nutrition* 100, no. 1 (July 2014): 437S–442S. doi.org/10.3945/ajcn.113.071472.

Michels, K. B., E. Giovannucci, A. T. Chan, R. Singhania, C. S. Fuchs, and W. C. Willett. "Fruit and Vegetable Consumption and Colorectal Adenomas in the Nurses' Health Study." *Cancer Research* 66, no. 7 (April 2006): 3942–53. doi.org/10.1158/0008-5472.CAN-05-3637.

NutritionFacts.org. "Beans." Accessed December 15, 2020. NutritionFacts.org/topics/beans.

Oliveira, Rosane. "Eat Your Beans!" UC Davis Integrative Medicine. July 3, 2016. PBLife.org/nutrition/eat-your-beans.

Surampudi, P., B. Enkhmaa, E. Anuurad, and L. Berglund. "Lipid Lowering with Soluble Dietary Fiber." *Current Atherosclerosis Reports* 18, no. 12 (December 2016): 75. doi.org/10.1007/s11883-016-0624-z.

White, Suzanne Caciola. *The Daily Bean.* Washington, DC: LifeLine Press, 2004.

Winham, Donna M., and Andrea M. Hutchins. "Perceptions of Flatulence from Bean Consumption among Adults in 3 Feeding Studies." *Nutrition Journal* 10 (November 2011): 128. doi.org/10.1186/1475-2891-10-128.

# Index

# Acknowledgments

Tony, thank you for being my number one supporter and always trying everything at least once. King and Zane, thank you for being my on-call taste testers.

Thanks to my parents for being a constant source of support and instilling in me a love of food and cooking and to all my family and friends around the world who have inspired me.

Thanks to Gleni Bartels and the whole team at Callisto for their support and encouragement.

# About the Author

**Katherine Green** is a writer and editor living in Portland, Oregon. She specializes in recipe development for special diets and has a certificate in nutritional therapy and a bachelor's degree in journalism. She is a fermentation enthusiast, home winemaker, and former owner of Mama Green's Jam. Follow her cooking and gardening adventures at HomeCookedPDX.com.

CPSIA information can be obtained
at www.ICGtesting.com
Printed in the USA
JSHW030820270421
13902JS00002B/5